PRIMITIVE
OUTDOOR
SKILLS

Richard L. Jamison

Third Printing: July 1992

International Standard Book Number
0-88290-263-6

Library of Congress Card Catalog Number
84-082234

Horizon Publishers' Catalog and Order Number
1234

Printed and distributed
in the United States of America by

Horizon
Publishers
& Distributors, Incorporated
P.O. Box 490 Bountiful, Utah 84011-0490

About the Authors

Ron (Gus) Gustaveson is an accomplished craftsman who has studied primitive skills for more than twenty years. His interest in ethnology and archaeology has prompted experimentation and development of many useful techniques which he has shared in his classes and workshops. Ron is currently compiling a book of the experiences of "old time" settlers and explorers of the West and has been a regular contributor to *Woodsmoke Journal.*

Paul Hellweg serves on the faculty of California State University at Northridge where he teaches classes in backpacking, mountaineering, wilderness survival and basic flintknapping. Paul is also an accomplished free-lance writer. His publications include more than two dozen articles appearing in national magazines and a book titled "Flintknapping, The Art of Making Stone Tools" which is available from Canyon Publishers, 8561 Eatough Avenue, Canoga Park, California 91304.

Linda Jamison has participated in many primitive expeditions, both as a student and as an instructor. She has conducted field trips and lectured on wild plant identification and use at the University of Southern Colorado, University of Colorado, Pikes Peak Community College and to many clubs and organizations. Linda is the managing editor of *Woodsmoke Journal* and a published free-lance writer.

Richard Jamison is a noted outdoor expert who has received national recognition for his skill in primitive craftsmanship and knowledge of aboriginal skills. Richard is also widely known as an outdoor photographer and writer. He has filmed and produced a series of ten outdoor educational films which are used by other instructors in schools throughout the United States and Europe. As director of Anasazi Expeditions he has conducted numerous primitive expeditions over the past fifteen years, accumulating an impressive "trail time." Richard is editor and publisher of *Woodsmoke Journal.*

Rich Johnson was the first editor of *Woodsmoke Journal* in 1978. A proficient mountaineer and outdoorsman, Rich, with his wife and two children, spent a year living a wilderness life style (primarily in a cave) while he evaluated and researched various survival techniques. He has written a book about his experiences as well as other survival-oriented articles. He is currently editor of a national magazine.

Larry Dean Olsen, author of the best-selling book "Outdoor Survival Skills," originated the award-winning "480" 30-day survival trek at Brigham Young University. He has been a pioneer in instigating primitive survival courses as an effective rehabilitation program in the United States. Larry has lectured and taught primitive survival throughout the nation.

Jim Riggs is an intense student of the early native American people and other aboriginal cultures. He has a degree in anthropology. As a result of his superb craftsmanship, and knowledge of the primitive life style of the early Great Basin people, he has been invited to contribute his work to the Oregon High Desert Museum. Jim conducts aboriginal life-style expeditions for the Malheur and Wallowa field stations in Oregon. He is also an accomplished artist, illustrator, and writer. His book "Blue Mountain Buckskin" is an authoritative work on the Indian brain-tanning method of making buckskin. (This is available by writing to "Blue Mountain Buckskin," Rt. 1, Box 44 E., Wallowa, Oregon 97885.)

Ernest and Margaret Wilkinson raise many wild animals including cougars, wolves, coyotes, badgers, bobcats, and a porcupine. They have acquired great knowledge about and love of nature and wildlife. Ernest is a nationally known outdoor photographer, writer, and lecturer. He was the principal photographer for the film "Cougar Country" which featured his own mountain lion, Tabby. Ernest and his ever-present wife and sidekick, Margaret, run a successful taxidermy shop. Both are expert instructors. Ernest has worked as a government trapper for many years in San Luis Valley of southern Colorado. Ernest and Margaret have written numerous articles which have appeared in national magazines. Currently they have a book (in the process of publication) which details many of Ernest's wilderness experiences.

Samantha Beckett-Windborn is a teacher by profession and an avid student of anthropology and native American history. She is an expert craftsperson, specializing in primitive pottery which she manufactures from native raw clays. Samantha has attended a number of primitive expeditions and has instructed classes at workshops for many years. She is a regular contributor to *Woodsmoke Journal*.

Contents

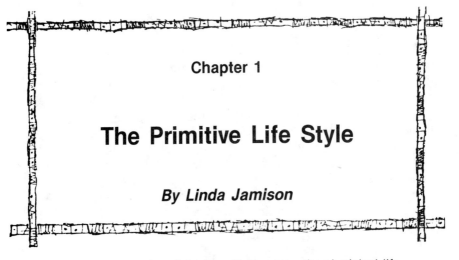

Chapter 1

The Primitive Life Style

By Linda Jamison

"It is this energy/result factor which causes the aboriginal life style to be attractive. It offers the satisfaction of simplifying life's efforts and allows us to see, feel, smell, and enjoy the fruits of our labors . . . immediately."

Part I

There is nothing elaborate about the aboriginal life style: it is a grand circle of life inseparable with nature; a chain of action which begins with the gathering of materials to make tools which are used to manufacture weapons and domestic wares, which make possible the use of the materials.

In this life style each contrivance has a usefulness. There are no unnecessary items to litter or move from place to place. In stark contrast, the last time we moved from one location to another we spent four days just packing and throwing out useless accumulations.

The aborigine sees, on all sides, the products of his own making. From the clothing he wears to the food he eats, these domestic skills fill the most basic needs of his people.

By comparison, the closest modern man comes to being totally self-sufficient is when he plants a garden. But even that would probably be abandoned if it were not for rototillers, fertilizers, ready-packaged seeds, garden hoses and sprinklers, not to mention canning jars, dehydrators, and freezers needed to preserve the harvest.

Our modern technology leaves us free to go to school, to work at a satisfying occupation of our choice, to develop our artisitic abilities, and even to go to the moon. It provides us with comfort, satisfaction, and a full stomach . . . but not with domestic security.

Not only don't most people create their domestic tools, because of the complexities, they cannot. If you look around, you will most likely find that not one of the "things" that make your life livable is the manufacture of your own hands.

True security comes from knowing that you are providing your own needs: you have learned to make soap from yucca; you can cook food on a rock or skewer; weave footwear from fibers on the spot as the need arises; make glue from pitch. Only with such skills will you truly enjoy the prosperity and comfort of our modern society.

If we can reduce our elaborate world to the simple chain of cause and effect that links us with nature, understand it, live with it, and respect it—then we will have earned the right to all that nature provides.

Part Ii

It is a proven fact that the "primitive experience" develops self-confidence, security, and an inner peace. But have you considered the formula required for this transformation?

One possibility is the direct and immediate satisfaction which is a result of physical and mental achievement.

For instance, the farmer sees many immediate results of his energy output in everyday life: when he plows a field he can see his freshly plowed field; when he chops wood, he has the satisfaction of a full wood shed.

Conversely, many people never actually *see* the results of their energy output. An office worker whose job is one of many in a long line of paper shufflers may never see the culmination of his efforts even though they are important to the overall success of the business.

In the business world we deal not only with factors that are virtually out of our control, but with elements that are, for us, "untouchable" such as corporate decisions, inflation, and politics.

No wonder our shelves are full of pills and our stomachs full of ulcers.

It is this energy/result factor which causes the aboriginal life style to be attractive. It offers the satisfaction of simplifying life's efforts and allows us to see, feel, smell, and enjoy the fruits of our labors . . . immediately.

The more we can pare our lives to the simple "abo existence" of energy/result dimensions, the less stress-ridden our lives will become and the more peace and self-satisfaction we will find.

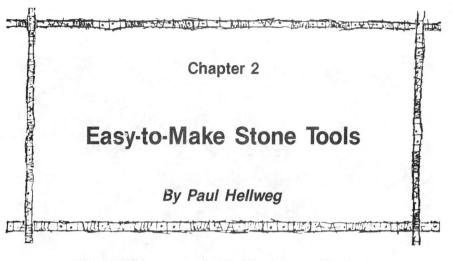

Chapter 2

Easy-to-Make Stone Tools

By Paul Hellweg

"It is possible . . . to make obsidian knives with edges sharper than the finest surgical steel."

Stone tools are frequently desirable and occasionally essential in survival situations. Their functions are limited only by the scope of the user's imagination—they help scrape hides, dress game, make fire sets, prepare cordage, and so forth. Unfortunately, stone tool-making is usually discussed as a technical skill similar to that of pressure or percussion flaking. These are highly desirable skills to acquire, and many students justifiably seek to master them. But these techniques may be of little or no use in an emergency. They are skills which require considerable practice to master; they will work only on siliceous minerals which frequently are not available; and they require flaking tools of antler, bone, or hardwood (which may also be unavailable).

I'll grant that a skilled flintknapper can create tools which are not only aesthetically pleasing but also pre-eminitely functional (it is possible, for example, to make obsidian knives with edges sharper than the finest surgical steel), but for the average survivalist the odds are against being able to make serviceable pressure or percussion-flaked tools in an emergency.

I would thus like to introduce a few techniques of stone tool manufacture that have none of the disadvantages discussed above. The techniques are: the Oldowan bashee; bi-polar percussion; and the discoidal knife. These methods of stoneworking require no previous practice, need no tools to aid manufacture, and can be done with a wide variety of stone. Most important, they are functional. Using these techniques, a totally unskilled person can make serviceable tools in a matter of minutes.

If a stream cobble is struck forcefully while resting on an anvil rock, the cobble will shear neatly in half. Ideally, your selected cobble should be about half the size of the one pictured. (An overly large stone is shown in the photo in order to emphasize the technique).

Oldowan Bashee Technology

Two and a half million years ago, what are considered by some to be man's predecessors, were making pebble choppers in the Olduvai region (Oldoway in German) of East Africa. But for countless millennia before the development of chopper tools, stone tool technology must have been pathetically crude. It probably involved picking up any old rock, heaving it mightily against another rock or boulder, and dimly hoping that this bashing would produce useful pieces. Any archaeologist worth his safari hat would scoff at me, but I cannot resist the urge to name this earliest possible tool-making culture. Thus, we have the "Oldowan Bashee" technology.

When this is applied to the manufacture of stone tools for survival, the Oldowan Bashee falls in the same category as covering your head when it's cold—the idea is so obvious that it is frequently overlooked. But now that the bashee has been named and written about, we have no excuse for overlooking this type of tool-making.

Oldowan Bashee tools: The fourteen pieces shown are the result of one "bashing" of an obsidian nodule. Most of the pieces have at least one sharp cutting edge.

Bashee tools are not very imposing, and they are not likely to be displayed to friends. But they are functional, and they can be extremely useful in emergencies. Almost any rock—fist-sized or smaller—will suffice. Ideally, it should be hard (quartzite is perfect) and it should have thin, crack-lines visible. You can easily pick out the harder rocks; their surfaces are smoother and less grainy. Also, they will feel comparatively heavy for their size. If the rocks are already cracked, they will shatter much more readily. Be sure to duck your head when you throw lest you be hit in the face or eye by bashee fragments. The resulting pieces, or bashee tools, will have sharp edges if the original rock was hard enough. These pieces will cut leather, dress small game, and so forth.

Bi-polar Percussion

Bi-polar percussion is a uniquely satisfying technique for working stone. It requires no more skill than does the Oldowan Bashee, but it leaves one with the proud feeling of actually making a tool. The technique is used to split a cobble. Without any previous practice, the survivalist should be able to shear a cobble cleanly in half. The separate halves make superb scrapers and they often provide good cutting edges.

A cobble of proper size has been neatly cut in half using bi- polar percussion.

Edge view of a cobble split with bi-polar percussion. Note the lipped edge on the left.

To accomplish the bi-polar technique, select a hard, roundish stream cobble of about fist-size, or slightly larger. Set the cobble upright on an anvil rock, then strike the cobble sharply on its top. The blow must be forceful, and it must be directed straight down upon the cobble. The force generated by the blow travels through the cobble, hits the anvil rock, and then rebounds upon itself. Since the force thus comes from both ends (or poles) of the cobble, the technique is known as bi-polar percussion. If properly executed, the result is a neatly sheared rock.

The skill involved is not in the execution of the technique, but in the selection of the proper cobble. The most common mistake is to select a rock too large to split handily. The cobble must be only about fist-size, and it should be free of cracks. A properly selected cobble will split with surprising ease, and the fracture will be slightly lipped at both ends. The lipped portions will, typically, be sharp enough to cut leather or dress small game (see photographs). These split cobbles are not only functional, they are also aesthetic. Unlike bashee tools, cleanly split cobbles are sometimes displayed proudly to friends and fellow survivalists.

Discoidal Knives

Discoidal refers to an object that is disk-shaped; that is, roundish and flatish. Discoidal knives are difficult to manufacture, sometimes frustratingly so. However, the technique is not complicated, and it does not really need to be practiced in advance. As in bi-polar percussion, the key to making discoidal knives lies in the selection of a suitable pebble.

To get started, select several small pebbles about two or three inches across. They should be round, flat, hard, and of smooth texture. Unfortunately, the range of stones that will work is much more restricted than is the case for bashee or bi- polar technology—basalt, chalcedony, chert, and flint would be the best choices, if they are available. If a pebble seems promising, the only real test is to give it a try. Hold the pebble securely in one hand and strike its edge sharply against another rock. The intent is to strike small flakes off the pebble's edge. But, in order to do this, it is imperative that the pebble be struck with as much force as can be mustered (keeping fingers carefully out of the way, of course).

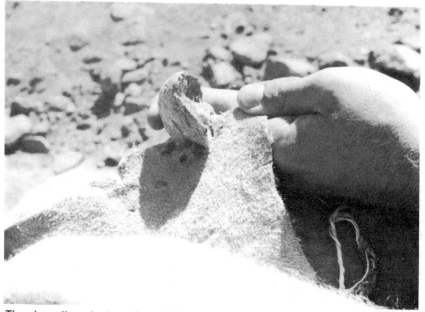

The sharp lipped edge of a cobble split with bi-polar percussion can be used to cut leather or other material.

A small basaltic stream pebble is being struck forcefully against another rock with the intent of striking off a discoidal knife.

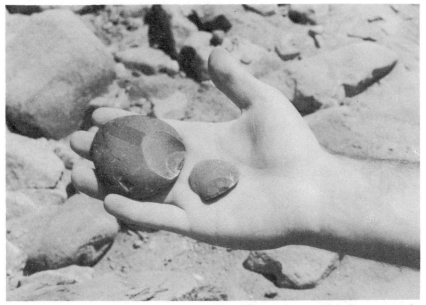

A discoidal knife and the "parent" pebble of basalt from which it was struck.

Expect quite a few failures at first, but you should eventually be striking off flakes which are round, flat, and have sharp edges; i.e., discoidal knives. These knives will be small, averaging about an inch in diameter. But their edges are extremely sharp; these little knives will cut meat, leather, or almost anything you would want a knife to cut.

Admittedly, manufacturing discoidal knives will take some practice, but the practice does not have to be in the form of a previously learned skill. It can be accomplished on the spot, in a survival situation. Besides, if your selected pebble refuses to yield up a discoidal knife, you can always resort to the Oldowan Bashee technique. This not only sends the offending pebble to its just reward, but also assuages one's damaged ego by clearly establishing who's boss. All that, plus you'll have some bashee tools.

And tools, if you'll remember, are what we were after in the first place.

Chapter 3

SWAMP CRAFT

By Richard Jamison

*"... we toted our bulrush boat home on top of the car—
ignoring the haughty stares of a caravan of honest-to-goodness
boating enthusiasts pulling their giant cabin-crusiers
and inboards."*

A sixty-mile trip with a bulrush boat attached to the top of our car drew a lot of attention. But few people understand the whys and where-fores of any of my projects, including my neighbors, who suspect that anyone who collects useless tree limbs (bow staffs,) rocks (axe heads), weeds (basket and cordage material), and old animal hides and feet must be a fool!

My "fool's paradise," about sixty miles south of our home, is the destination of an annual fall excursion to collect basket and weaving material. There the bulrush (Scirpus) grows to be twelve feet high and it is easy to get to within a few feet of the road. On one particular occasion we planned a boat-building project.

I had taken a group of students to this spot for a similar outing earlier in the year. It was much colder so I hadn't planned to test the boats, but one of the boys got so excited he peeled off his shirt, rolled up his trousers and plunged into the icy water with boat in tow. He pad-dled a few feet to prove the craft's sea-worthiness, then left the freez-ing water with a shivering, blue-lipped grin of satisfaction.

It is exciting to create a thing of craftsmanship absolutely from beginning to end, and it is hard to leave it behind, even though modern living has no utilitarian purpose for such things. That explains why we toted our bulrush boat home on top of the car—ignoring the haughty stares of a caravan of honest-to-goodness boating enthusiasts whose cars pulled giant cabin-cruisers and inboards.

21

The building of a bulrush boat can be a rewarding project as well as a useful mode of transportation through calm waterways and swampy areas, but not necessarily in the winter. The rushes are less than perfect for boat-building then. Also the boat tends to "list" as it becomes waterlogged and might very well cause you to take a cold dip.

But the boat can be used for human transport, and it also serves as an excellent raft for carting game or materials through or across water.

Materials

Almost any plant with a long slender stem and a pithy center can be used for raft material; some are just more suited to that use than others. The bulrush is my first choice. It's inner pith is much like styrofoam. The long leaves, often twelve feet or more, are exceptionally easy to work with. A bundle of three of four armsfull will give you enough material to make a small boat.

I sometimes mistakenly assume that most people know how to identify bulrush and where to find it, but unless you are involved in

The inner pith of bulrush (Scirpus) is much like styrofoam and is quite bouyant.

weaving or boat building, or even home decorating with dried weeds and things, such knowledge is not apt to be on top of your list of "important things to learn."

The most common error of identification seems to be mistaking cattail for bulrush. The easiest way I know to tell one from the other is by the seed formations. Cattail seeds form on top of the stems like large, brown sausages and often remain during the winter months. The dark brown seeds of the bulrush dangle from the ends of the stems like tassles in the wind. Another way to tell the difference is by the shape of the leaf; cattail leaves are knife-like, long and slender while the leaf of the bulrush is long, and as round as a pencil. Also, bulrushes are often a darker green than are the cattail leaves.

Both cattails and bulrushes grow in drainages and swampy areas. Often they are easily accessible along railroad tracks where water collects in the ditches and on the banks of waterways. I have seldom found it necessary to wade through swamps in order to find good specimens.

Cattail (Typha) leaves can be used for boat building, but the slender shape of the leaves means less inner pith, which greatly increases the quantity of material needed for each project.

South American Indians make beautiful boats from reed grass (Phragmites). Thor Heyerdahl's original "RA" was made of reeds and that craft proved to be quite durable and bouyant.

Bulrush Gathering

Bulrushes are gathered seasonally, usually at the height of the growing season—early fall or late summer. We gather large bundles at this time of year, dry them and choose the best to keep for basket projects. There is little use in collecting poor specimens, or in taking up storage space with material that will only be discarded later. Any leaves that have rust spots (dark brown splotches) should be discarded because they are weak places in the leaf which will break, or tear, when you don't want or expect them to.

For this particular project we cut about four armloads of bulrush leaves and spread them evenly in a cool shady spot under a large tree. Fresh rushes are too brittle to use; they will crack when they are tied tightly and they soak up water more readily. It would be foolish to take the time and effort necessary to complete a project and have a useless finished product because the materials you chose were inferior.

That's not to say you absolutely cannot use fresh rushes for your boat, but it is better to begin with rushes collected and dried earlier, then dampened again for the project.

Large amounts of bulrush can be gathered in the fall before rust spots appear, dried, and used for winter projects.

Braid plenty of rush "rope" before you begin your project so it will be on hand as you work.

You will learn to know at what stage of drying the plants will be ready to begin your boat building. I recommend testing the leaf by squeezing it between your fingers. It should be "spongy" not brittle. If it "cracks" when you squeeze it, it is either too fresh or it has been soaked too long.

If you are using dry bulrushes to make a boat you will have to dampen them first, but be careful not to *soak* them; waterlogged rushes will crack just as too-fresh leaves will. They are also more easily affected by rust. The best way to dampen the leaves is to sprinkle them with water and wrap them in a damp cloth for a couple of hours, then draw out a few from the center of the sheath which will leave the rest protected from the moisture-sapping air.

You will need enough braided rushes to wrap around the body of the boat and to securely tie the two sections together. If you expect your boat to last, use braided rushes for all binding, especially in areas that will be under the most stress. Three bulrush leaves braided together are remarkably strong and durable. Because it is necessary to have one long, continuous strand of cordage, be sure to splice at alternate points to avoid weak points. Just tie off the braid at the end.

Bundle the rushes evenly by alternating the long and short rushes so the body of the bundles will be approximately the same diameter.

You can also use hand-twisted, two-ply cordage but it takes quite a long time to make. I prefer to just twist two leaves together.

Technique

Begin to make your swamp craft by bundling the rushes evenly. This is done by alternating long and shorter leaves so that the 'body' will be about the same diameter. The front—or bow—of the boat should taper to approximately half the diameter of the body; this section should be about three feet long and the body six feet.

Next, tie the body securely with a double-wrap of braided cordage and the bow with a double-twisted wrap. Slip the knot of the binding on the body to one side so that the tie will lay between the two sections. Seperate about one-fourth of the rushes in the bow, pull them up and wrap them tightly with a twist of cordage. This will hold the other rushes up and form the bow of the boat; otherwise all you will have is a raft.

Make another section the same size as the first, then bind the sterns tightly together with a double wrap of braid. Tie the bow sections together by "sewing" through the rushes.

Once the sections are bound together securely, the uneven stems at the stern can be trimmed. This is for appearance only, it's strange enough to travel down the road with a bulrush boat on top of the car; you certainly don't want it to look tacky!

Next, a ring, or lip, is added to the main section of the boat. Its purpose is not to prevent water from lapping over the sides, but to form an edge so that game, or other loads, can be easily carried on the boat. This will also help you to stay on top of the boat, not always an easy task. The lip is made by alternating rushes into a uniform sheaf and tying it with a continuous wrap of twine or braided cordage of rushes. Then tie the lip in place by sewing it through the wrap, and the rushes, in the main section of the boat.

Unless you plan to lay on top of the boat and paddle it with your hands you will need a long, sturdy pole with which to propel yourself in shallow waterways. In deep water you will need a paddle. Be sure to launch the boat in shallow water so you can board from the stern. It is rather humorous to see someone trying to get on top of a bulrush boat after they have capsized in deep water, they look like they are climbing on top of a large !og. To avoid capsizing sit on top of the boat on your knees and adjust your weight carefully toward the center back.

Raise and wrap a small bundle of the "bow" section.

Pull the rest of the rushes up and tie them with several twists of wrap.

Proper Care

The boat will eventually take on water and, depending on the weight of the load and the "list" of the craft, can only be used for a couple of hours before it must be taken out to dry again. But if it is well made and given proper care it can serve you for many months. Proper care includes keeping the boat dry when you're not using it by beaching it

When you have two identical bundles complete, turn the knots to the inside and bind the bundles tightly by "sewing" through the rushes.

on logs or some other base that allows air to circulate beneath it. Otherwise it will mildew quickly, and rust spots will deteriorate the rushes.

A finished bulrush boat is lightweight and can easily be carried by one person (when it is dry). Conversely, a wet, soggy boat can be incredibly heavy and difficult to beach. You will need to let it "drain" a bit before hauling it out to dry.

All things considered, I sincerely feel that learning to build a bulrush craft—and I have built many—has been one of my most rewarding projects. I doubt that I will ever take an extended trip on one, but I recommend that you know the technique if a need does arise. You are far less likely to find logs for building a raft to cross swampy areas and shallow waterways than you are to find rushes or cattails.

The looks on the faces of the motorists we passed while bringing our swamp craft home was a bonus we hadn't expected.

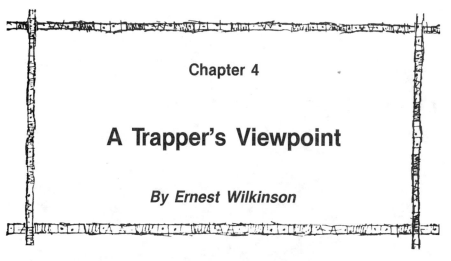

Chapter 4

A Trapper's Viewpoint

By Ernest Wilkinson

"Trapping is similar to harvesting a wheat crop, or trimming animals from a grazing herd of sheep or cattle each year."

Are you remorseful when you hear a conversation concerning trapping, or when you see a person wearing a fur coat?

Some folks advocate the use of fake furs. Give that some thought. Fake fur is made from petroleum by-products which are a non-renewable resource. Natural furs, however, are like crops—a renewable resource every year when properly harvested.

I have discovered that many people, these days, resent trapping, but after further research I find that most of those who would like to have trapping outlawed in various states do not fully understand the principles of wildlife management, nor the true habits of wildlife. They have probably seen too many TV shows or read too many news stories that present slanted opinions and foster falsehoods.

With this in mind I would like to clarify a few facts about the trapping of some fur bearers and then allow you to form your own opinion.

Perhaps you have bought or leased a piece of land on which you are attempting to raise chickens, sheep, or other livestock as meat for your own use, or to sell, then coyotes begin to move in from surrounding brush country and carry off your chickens or kill your sheep. If this continues unchecked you will soon be out of business. Depending on your financial circumstances, you may be forced to move or lose your property.

Since the coyote has very few natural enemies, aside from man, and since they have fairly large litters of four to ten pups whelped in April or May of each year, their numbers can increase quite rapidly.

Avid wildlife photographer and outdoors expert Ernest Wilkinson takes a stroll with his pet mountain lion and badger.

By fall most of the pups are grown up enough to start hunting on their own, so where you had a single pair of coyotes in the spring you now have eight to ten, or more, adult coyotes in the fall. You can fully realize the fast growth in coyote population when spring again arrives and those eight, ten, or more coyotes pair off and and whelp more pups.

The predator has to be stopped, either by shooting the guilty animals or by trapping them. Since coyotes nearly always hunt at night, when you can't see to shoot them, trapping is the best solution to the problem.

You can generally take about seventy percent of the coyotes in a given area each winter and still maintain the same population level year after year. When the coyote population does get high, the number of bobcats, fox, and other species of wildlife goes down. There are people who blame the hunting and trapping pressure for this decrease yet, in reality, winter and feed conditions, along with other factors, determine the wildlife population far more than trapping pressure does.

Control Animal Population

For example, a square mile of land along a creek bottom that contains water with crawdads, frogs, with brush and hollow logs for shelter, with perhaps a nearby corn field for added food, will support about twenty-five raccoons. An adjoining square mile of land, with no proper habitat, might support only one or two. In the spring, when the young raccoons grow up, the increased population must move on to another area or die of slow starvation, disease, or cannibalism. It's much like stuffing beans into a jar; when the jar is full, it will hold no more and the overflow must be moved. Thus trapping usually helps to keep the animal population under control with a healthier base population rather than allowing nature to take it's course through starvation, or worse.

The same principle applies to beaver. At one time, the beaver was in trouble because of the mountainman who opened up the West in quest of beaver pelts for the fur trade, yet did not leave enough of the animals for "seed." About the time conservation came into being, the beaver population was extremely low and most states gave them complete protection. Since they are very prolific, beaver soon made a rapid comeback. They are even a nuisance, in some areas, when their dam building activities result in flooded crops and roads.

Toward fall, when a pair of beaver locate a suitable water habitat, they begin to deepen the channels and build dams to deepen the water so it won't freeze solid during the winter. They cut many willows, alder and similar trees and pile them into a food cache in deep water. Then, when everything is frozen during the winter, they swim under the ice to their food cache, grasp a limb, and carry it into the lodge where they chew off the bark and discard the wood core.

Two to four or more baby beaver appear in the spring and stay with the older pair through the next winter, and into the spring, when a second batch of babies comes along. Sometime during the second summer the "yearlings" are pushed out. They have to find their own area and begin their own dam and lodge.

These yearlings are not allowed to move in with another colony up or down the waterway, and if the stream is full of established beaver or the food supply depleted, where do they go?

When a beaver is moved during the fall of the year it usually doesn't have time to locate a suitable area and get a food cache stored up before winter sets in. Therefore, it faces a slow death by starvation during a harsh winter, or it may become weak from continual battles with established beaver so that it is easily overtaken by predators when searching out a suitable home. Sometimes these roving beaver settle in areas where they are not welcome, such as near homes and cabins.

I used to live-trap quite a few beaver myself, and transport them away from the damage area to some stream in the mountains that could make a home for them. But now many of those streams have an overpopulation of beaver, so there is no point in live-trapping any longer.

Controlled trapping is similar to harvesting a wheat crop, or trimming animals from a grazing herd of sheep or cattle each year. If certain animals are not harvested a valuable resource is wasted or the quality of the other livestock is destroyed.

Ernest believes that trapping animals that become too numerous for the area is the most humane method of control. Here he resets his traps after a successful catch.

Chapter 5

Ancient Steam-Pit Cooking

By Rich Johnson

" . . . the Cochise culture of the (American) southwest used the steaming pit as a cooking method, and archaeologists believe that the Cochise were around over 10,000 years ago."

What if, for some reason, all electricity and natural gas suddenly became unavailable? Or, what if we were all forced to flee from the conveniences of city life and leave behind our kitchen appliances? Or, what if . . . for some reason we should just want to get up and abandon the hectic "good life" of our modern age, and start living the "real life" in a more pioneer setting? Under any of these conditions we would have to learn new ways to perform old duties such as cooking. The "new ways" would really be ancient or primitive ways when compared with recent technology. In the quest for alternative sources of energy, and energy conservation there is something to be learned from primitive methods.

Our family has used a primitive technique for cooking meat and vegetables for many seasons, and the only energy it uses is that provided by burning a few dead sticks. This is the ancient "steaming pit" that has been used by many different peoples around the world for thousands of years.

History of the Pit

Indeed, right here in the United States, the Cochise culture of the southwest used the steaming pit as a cooking method, and archaeologists believe that the Cochise people were around over 10,000 years ago. On the other hand, today you can travel to Hawaii and enjoy a luau where the main course is cooked in a pit by this same old technique.

35

The first part of the steaming pit project is digging the pit. The dimensions of the hole depend on the size and amount of food to be cooked.

The way I look at it, any procedure that has withstood the test of time for over 10,000 years must have some merit.

The principle employed in pit cookery is slow, even heat that is completely sealed against escape. In this way the natural juices and the flavor of the food are locked in during the cooking process instead of being driven off. And, since the pit is gradually cooling off as the food is being cooked, there is no danger of burning the offerings.

How to Build Yours

To build your own pit oven, find a spot of ground and clear away any flammable materials for a distance of about eight to ten feet. The pit itself (unless you're doing a genuine Hawaiian luau) will only be about two feet wide, three feet long, and one foot deep, so you're really not sacrificing much land for this project.

Dig out the hole according to the dimensions listed above, trying all the while to maintain fairly vertical walls along the edges. Be sure to pile all of the dirt as near the excavation as possible without allowing it to fall back into the pit. This is because you will be using the soil to help seal in the heat for the cooking time.

After the crater is completed you will need to find a supply of fairly flat rocks with which to line the pit. Lining the pit doesn't mean just putting down a floor, but it means floor and walls both. The rocks you choose should be as flat as possible, but other shapes will serve the same purpose. The only drawback to round rocks is that they take up more room in the pit, and you may want to enlarge it to make up for the lost space if you use rocks with obnoxious shapes. Select your rocks from somewhere other than a stream bed, because stones that have been in the water for a long time can trap a small amount of moisture inside, and when heated they could explode.

Now that you have "tiled" the floor and walls of your new oven, you are ready to build a small fire to heat the rocks. The fire should be laid so as to warm up the entire length and width of the pit, and should be kept relatively small. By that I mean you don't have to heat up the whole outdoors, just the rocks in the oven. Use hardwoods if at all possible, because they will give you the best bed of coals and will burn the hottest and longest. The blaze should be kept alive for about forty-five minutes to an hour, and the coals will keep the pit hot for quite a while longer while you make final preparations to the food.

After the fire has burned long enough to sufficiently heat the stone, remove the coals from the oven and add plenty of wild foliage such as grass or other "edible" greens as insulation from the hot stones.

Other Preparations

When you have your eatables all set for the fireworks, you will need to remove as many of the coals as possible from the interior of the pit. With the coals removed, the hot-stone lining is exposed and ready to do its work. These rocks are now sufficiently warm to fry eggs upon, so they would also be capable of burning the dinner unless some precautions are taken. The accepted practice among people who use fire-pit cooking is to wrap the food in some kind of insulating material such as green grass, large "edible" leaves, or other green food plants. (It's important to make sure that you don't use poisonous plants for this purpose. It is not a difficult task to learn which plants are edible and which are poisonous in your area.) Of course you could always use tin foil, but the flavor isn't the same as if you used watercress, for example, or curley dock, or dandelion as your insulating layer.

But whatever you use, use plenty. Lay a thick layer on the stone floor, then place the victuals on this, and finally lay another heavy layer over the top. At this point you will want to sprinkle about a cup of water over the whole thing to help produce steam during the cooking period.

Now seal it all up with some slabs of bark or anything else that will help keep the dirt from sifting through to the food, and place this over the top layer of greenery. Then quickly bury the entire thing under about four inches of soil, and go do something else for about three hours. When you return, your dinner will be ready. After a treatment like this, rabbit and chicken literally fall off the bones, and they are a tender, juicy delight to munch on.

I have to admit that our first attempt to use the steam-pit cooking technique was totally experimental even though we had some background knowledge about it. Our initial oven was large enough to cook a medium-sized cow, and we soon learned that, for our family of four, it doesn't really require that much space. A pit about three times the size of the total amount of food to be placed in it is about right. I have even cooked a whole chicken in a pit not much larger than the chicken itself. This part is pretty flexible, but you don't want to do a lot of unnecessary digging. By the same token, we have used a fairly large oven to prepare small meals by simply partitioning off the area we are not going to use with a pile of dirt, while building the fire in the section we do want to use.

It is best to cut large pieces of meat into smaller pieces so it will cook more thoroughly, and faster. Large game birds can be cooked by placing a few small heated stones inside the body cavity during the cooking time.

With the steam inside doing its job, you must seal the oven so the heat won't escape. Bark slabs, a large rock, or piece of material such as a burlap bag can be used. The main purpose is to keep the soil out of the food when you seal the pit.

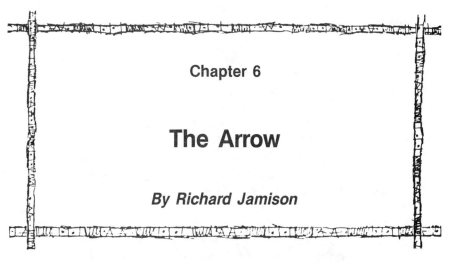

Chapter 6

The Arrow

By Richard Jamison

" . . . the bow is only half the weapon; the arrow must be of equal quality or it will not find it's mark no matter how powerful the bow or how talented the marksman."

The manufacture of weapons is not necessary for survival. There are methods of trapping game and fish that exceed the stalking techniques used in prehistoric and later times that are actually more efficient. Nevertheless, my enjoyment in the skills of weaponry increases in the pleasure of their creation. A well-made bow, a finely fletched arrow, a precisely balanced spear or atlatl are truly works of art.

Claude Levi-Strauss once said, "A primitive people is not a backward or retarded people; indeed they may possess a genius for invention or action that leaves the achievements of civilized people far behind."

One of these achievements was the invention of the bow and arrow, a landmark among primitives the world over. These "new, advanced" weapons enabled the hunter to kill big game from a greater distance by the use of increased velocity—far healthier than creeping up to stab the animal.

But the bow is only half the weapon; the arrow must be of equal quality or it will not find its mark no matter how powerful the bow or how talented the marksman. (Detailed instruction on the manufacture of the arrow "point" is covered in chapter 15 in the first volume of *The Best of Woodsmoke*.)

Arrow making, while relaxing in the cool shade of a cottonwood tree, is a rewarding way to spend a hot afternoon. There is a sense of accomplishment in each step of the process, from collecting the material to adding the final embellishment.

In constructing arrows, as with all skills, the "right" material for your project will depend on what grows in your geographical area. Rose (Rosa), ash (Fraxinus), willow (Salix), currant (Ribes), gooseberry (Ribes), cedar (Juniperus), and reed grass (Phragmites) are all good arrow-staff materials available in the Midwest. My own preferences are rose, currant, and reed grass.

Arrow shafts should be a minimum of three feet in length and about three-eighths-of-an-inch in diameter or slightly larger and as straight as possible. Once cut, the shafts should be bundled tightly and allowed to "season" for a week or more to thoroughly dry. If the bark is removed too soon, the wood may crack and split.

When they are dry, I peel the arrows and straighten them somewhat by rubbing them against a heated stone. Using a hot stone while I work keeps me away from the direct heat of the fire. If you prefer to work directly over a fire take care not to burn or scorch the wood. This will make it brittle.

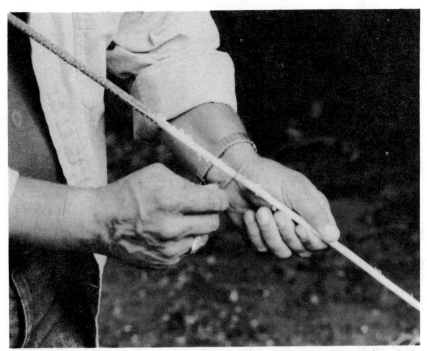

Once it is thoroughly dry, the rose shaft is carefully peeled before it is straightened.

Occasionally the shaft will have a "kink" that must be removed. Do this with an arrow wrench: a piece of stone, bone, or a wooden handle with a hole in it used to apply pressure on the crooked section of the shaft. I have also found that if I soak a piece of bark in water and wrap it around the crooked area, then heat it with a hot stone, stubborn spots will be straightened.

After a second straightening, scrape off any remaining bark and sand the arrow with two pieces of grooved sandstone placed on each side of the shaft. As a final step, the arrow can be polished for uniformity.

Length and Shaft

Measure the arrow before you cut it to its final length. The proper length will depend on your bow. The modern bow necessitates a longer arrow than its primitive counterpart . . . a factor which, by the way, has nothing to do with the strength of the bow. To use an arrow which is

The arrow shaft can most easily be straightened by rubbing it across a heated stone. This prevents burning or scorching the wood.

too long will cause "finger pinch"; the shorter the bow, the more the pinch. To come close to a proper length, place the shaft against the chest and extend the arms straight out along the shaft to the tip of the fingers where it should be cut off. My own arrows are twenty-six inches long when I use the above method or, when I use the Indian method of measuring, from the elbow to the tip of the index finger, adding the length from the wrist to the first joint of the middle finger.

Once the arrow shaft is cut to length a notch must be made into which the arrow point is placed. The notch is important because it provides a solid base for the point. If you merely split the end and insert the point, the shaft will split on impact.

Begin the notch by making two small cuts opposite one another on each side of the smallest end of the shaft, about three-quarters of an inch from the end. Next turn the shaft and make two more cuts about a quarter inch above the first ones. Now join the cuts with another short

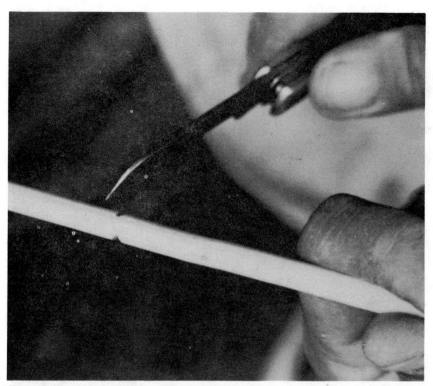

To make the notch, begin by making two small cuts opposite one another on the shaft.

incision and work the notch carefully until it splits. The loose end can then be removed and the edges sanded smooth so that the wood tapers down to the arrow point. This smooth surface will allow the arrow to penetrate more easily.

Heat the arrow shaft slowly in the warm ashes of your fire, then use a pitch, or glue stick, to apply a sticky binding agent to the notch by twirling the heated arrow shaft between your fingers. Next, heat some pitch mixed wih a small amount of charcoal. Place a soft ball of the mixture into the notch to hold the arrow point. Press the point securely into the pitched notch, then reinforce it by wrapping the notch and blunt end of the point smoothly with sinew. (See the article on the preparation and use of pitch in chapter 2, volume I, *The Best of Woodsmoke*.) Hide glue can also be used in place of pitch; a thick substance made by boiling rawhide, fish skin, and animal hooves.

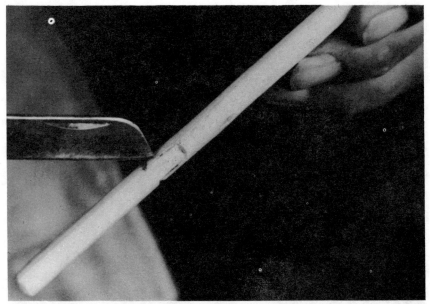

Turn the shaft and make two more cuts about one-quarter inch above the first cut. Join the cuts with a short incision.

Use a pitch stick to apply the binding agent to the heated arrow shaft.

The next step is to cut the "nock" in the opposite end of the arrow shaft. Nocking the shaft for the bowstring is done by sawing the end of the arrow with a piece of stone. The groove should be about one quarter-inch deep and "U" shaped, although some native American tribes used a "V" or other variations; it was possible to identify a particular tribe from their distinctive arrow nock.

Finally the fletching, or feathers, are added. An arrow is fletched to stabilize the shaft during flight.

Fletching

You can save a lot of trouble by having everything ready before you begin fletching. I like to sit near the fire, have my prepared feathers on my knee, my pitch stick within easy reach, and several strings of sinew strips in my mouth so they will be thoroughly wet before I heat the shaft.

Use feathers from the same wing to insure that the curve of the "rib" is the same. Prepare the feathers by straightening them. At home, I can pass the quill over a light bulb. In the field, I use a heated rock. While holding the feather at both ends, pass it back and forth over the

Reinforce the pitch with sinew (animal tendon) which has been dried and separated into small strands. Wet again to form a strong, tight bind.

Wrap the notched end of the arrow smoothly with wet sinew.

Once the feather has been straightened, split the midrib carefully down the middle.

hot stone until the feather is straight, then allow it to cool. This makes it easier to split the midrib accurately.

Three feathers are usually used in fletching, but arrows are sometimes made with only two. They are often deliberately spiraled, but usually the spiraling is natural, caused by the curve in the rib of the feather. A spiraled fletching (fluflu) is useful for hunting birds and small game because it allows the arrow to release quickly with more "spin," yet it won't travel as great a distance as the parallel fletched arrow.

Once the feather is carefully cut, the pith is removed by scraping the midrib as thin as possible. This allows the feather to lay flat against the arrow shaft.

Now measure the feather on the shaft so you will know where to apply the glue, or pitch. Don't cut the feathers to finished length; the extended ends will give you something to grasp as you pull the fletching tight before the sinew hardens.

To attach the feathers, you must first heat the shaft over the coals. Next, apply the glue or pitch directly to the shaft at the front point where the feathers will be attached and also at the rear, near the nock. I learned this the hard way. I applied pitch only to the front of the shaft,

Before attaching the feathers with pitch you must heat the shaft over the coals again.

then when I realized my mistake, I thought I could just pull the feathers back and heat the shaft again to apply the pitch on the end "after the fact." As you can probably imagine, it didn't work. The feathers caught fire and I had to start the fletching over again. So, while the glue is still soft, quickly press the quills of the feathers against the wood, arranging them on the shaft.

Some historians believe that fletching was aligned with the arrow-head and that if the arrow point was fired horizontally it would enter between the ribs of the animal. But since the arrow spins in flight there is no substance to this theory, and no particular reason to align the feathers to the arrow point. Some craftsmen simply prefer to do this.

In front of the feathers, to about one inch down the shaft, wrap the quill tips with sinew for a smooth finish. It is important to apply the sinew evenly to eliminate rough surfaces. My preference is to leave the "down" on the feathers for decoration.

Now attach the feathers to the shaft at the rear of the arrow. Since the pitch or glue that you applied before will be dry by this time the feathers won't "stick" to the shaft, but it will act as a binding agent

Wrap the quill tips with sinew about one inch up the shaft for a smooth, even finish.

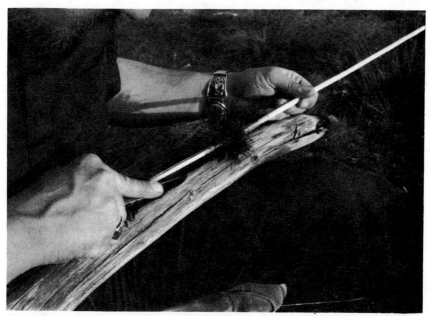

You may want to identify your arrows with an original style of trim or cresting.

when you add the sinew. You should trim the feathers from the quill at the point where the sinew will be wrapped to about one inch above the nock. Then moisten the feathers and smooth them "forward" while you apply the sinew. (This merely keeps feathers out of your way while you wrap.)

You can secure each quill separately, adding the next with each subsequent wrap until all three are in place. They should be loose enough that you can grasp the end of the feathers to align and pull them tight. (This is why you don't trim the feathers until the very end of the process.) Now tighten the sinew and trim off the excess length.

You may want to identify your arrows with an original style of cut feathers, cresting (dying the shaft with a specific design), or carving nicks or other distinguishing marks on the arrow itself. Originally this was done so there would be no question about who killed the game during a hunting party. When you finish a piece of workmanship that you are proud of, put your mark on it.

The manufacture of cane (Phragmites) arrows is slightly different from the method used for the solid shaft arrow. The cane stalk is straightened by heating each joint and bending it carefully. (A warm rock works well for this procedure.)

Making the Foreshaft

The hollow stalk of the cane requires a foreshaft which is inserted into the larger end of the shaft. I measure the length of the cane the same as I measure the solid shaft arrow, although the finished product will be six to eight inches longer by the time the foreshaft is added. If you cut the shaft down to compensate for this extra length you will find that, when you draw the bow, the connection where the foreshaft is inserted will surely drag across your hand and may cause an injury.

Unlike the solid arrow, the larger end of the cane is at the front and the smaller end is fletched. The front of the stalk is cut about four inches in front of the joint so that the hollow end is open to insert the foreshaft. The opposite end is cut about a half-inch behind the joint for the nock. Both ends are pitched and wrapped with sinew so that the stalk won't split.

Choose a foreshaft slightly smaller than the diameter of the stalk, then taper one end so that it will fit smoothly into the shaft. The length of the foreshaft is a matter of preference; it can be only two inches long or as long as six-inches. Although I shoot a relatively short (twenty-six inch) solid arrow, I generally cut the foreshafts about six to eight inches long for a cane arrow.

The foreshaft is notched as it is for the solid arrow, and the point is inserted and secured with pitch, or glue and sinew. The feathers are attached in the same way, and the nock cut and smoothed just below the joint.

The cane arrow is excellent for fishing. The foreshaft can be considerably longer, like a spear or harpoon, with a piece of cordage tied to it and, concurrently, to the arrow so that when the fish is speared you will be able to recover the arrow, foreshaft, and fish intact.

Some people have the idea that they must draw their bow the length of the arrow. The draw of the bow depends on where it begins to "stack" (the point at which it feels hard to pull). This will vary with the length of your bow. The length of the bow often dictates the length of the arrow as well. A short bow with a light, short arrow is every bit as powerful as a long, heavy bow with a long arrow.

The primitive arrow is not as precise as the modern fiberglass and aluminum arrows used by archers today (because of consistency of mechanization) but it gives the craftsman enough satisfaction for his effort; certainly it surpasses the modern arrow in beauty and, more importantly, in sense of accomplishment.

The cane arrow is fitted with a solid foreshaft. The length of the foreshaft is a matter of preference, but is usually about six inches.

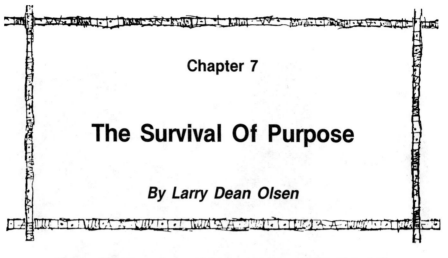

Chapter 7

The Survival Of Purpose

By Larry Dean Olsen

"One's ultimate goal should be to develop a self-sufficient life style with purpose that is mature, not forgetting that the dignity of work is the major ingredient."

Many people are reaching out into the country and into the wilderness for a re-identification with nature. At least one writer has said that this process amounts to an adolescent experience. Perhaps his reasoning lies in an observation made that many of these people have not yet gained a mature purpose for becoming self-sufficient.

Man, I believe, is a part of nature. If this is true, then it must follow that a part of man is sustained by the processes of natural living. Yet, too often, the attempt to capture a natural life style fails. Human potential is sometimes brought down to little more than a poverty performance. Let us look at some levels of desire for independence so that we may determine where the adolescent imagery gives way to a more mature view of man in nature and in society.

Level 1

George had finally thrown over higher education and decided that the "rat race" was too much to bear. He wanted to sweat with honest toil instead of sweating it out in the business world. So, with a determined will to become a back-to-the-lander, and with a sincere vow of poverty, he retreated.

Somewhere down the line, George gravitated from honest toil to shedding his educted sweat in some environmental or anti-corporate causes. Meanwhile, his own land stewardship became a veritable junkpile of so-called self-sufficient living. It included a "salvage dwelling" which would be energy efficient, someday; a weed-patch garden which might provide edibles for about ten percent of his yearly food needs; a well-stocked library; dirty overalls (just dirt, no sweat); and a book of food stamps.

Level 2

Dave also left the boundaries of civilization to seek a oneness with the natural world. He spent many weeks roaming the hills to find the secrets of life, identifiable to him through the literature he packed along. His quest was sincere and one that is needed from time to time by everyone. However, all direction was inward as Dave scooped up the lessons of nature, and he soon dwelt solely in his world of unspoiled beauty.

Level 3

Frank, out of concern for his urban-spoiled family, sold everything that fifteen years of hard work and keen wits had earned. He purchased his five acres, and independence, and moved to the country. Life style was important to Frank and his desire to sit and whittle soon gave way to serious sweat to get things going. He was partially self-sustaining so long as he sacrificed some time at a job in town, usually one outside his professional expertise. That was okay, though, and his only real frustration was in getting his family to make the shift from urban entertainment to country concerns for weather, weeding, and animal husbandry. Gradually, however, his long-standing drive and "umph" tempted him to dip his hand back into the business world. He innovated ideas, services, and even products which, through careful management, actually contributed to others.

In each of these three illustrations, the men had at least one motivation in common . . . escape. They fled to a state where the important lessons and feelings of nature could be introduced to them, perhaps for the first time. All three used an adolescent approach without any understanding of true independence, which should be the *major purpose* for self-sufficiency.

The survival of purpose means that one must constantly look at one's reason for stepping out of a cream-puff dependence into the sweaty world of self-sufficiency. There must be an awakening into a mature experience with self-reliant living.

What motivated George to accept a life of self-inflicted poverty? He had read about simple, but non-excess-producing societies which have current appeal, and he believed that the purpose of life lay somewhere in that unstressful atmosphere. He unwittingly placed himself in the same dominated and dependent condition found in almost every poverty-level group around the globe, and he is wide open to manipulation by governments and even by some radical pressure groups. He is actually far from being self-sufficient, even with his land and garden.

Dave may be better off, since—as a wanderer—he possesses more freedom. But ultimately, if he makes it a permanent affair with nature, his lack of stewardship will restrict his ability to build a more settled and contributing life style later on. He may simply become another interesting, and perhaps colorful, person for others to talk to in justifying their own deep longings to escape.

Frank may bust himself eventually unless his purpose is born of the strictest resolve. His return to what he considers the "rat race" would be inevitable if his original motive was only to escape. On the other hand, if his major motive was to purposely eliminate the traps of that rat race, then his chances for survival in a new life style are greater.

One's ultimate goal should be to develop a self-sufficient life style with purpose that is mature, not forgetting that the dignity of work is the major ingredient.

Level 4

Now let's look at another level of independence, with Victor. His desire to become more self-reliant is longstanding, and his life has reflected some wise restraint in that process. Itemized, his efforts look something like this:

a. He has become educated formally and also through a continuing program of independent study, apprenticeships, and practical experiences.

b. He has developed a useful, progressive, but undemeaning profession wich enables him to be financially self-sustaining as well. He is able to keep his profession alive and interesting without sacrificing his family ideals or his life style.

c. He allows for contingencies in the happy perspective of survival on the land by continually looking at his purpose for doing so. He knows the value of certain societal offerings which include a wise insurance program, proper medical protection and immunization, etc.

d. He maintains a fiercely won freedom from debt and from any dependency on agencies that may try to offer him assistance in the form of food stamps, free health clinics, price supports, grants in aid, public welfare, and any other monetary assistances. He shuns the dole in all its forms, thus maintaining his self-respect and freedom from the dependencies.

e. He has built for his own family a system of preparedness for the unforseen problems of poor health, occasional sickness, a lost job, natural emergencies, and possible social or man-made emergencies. To accomplish this he stores away, in an efficient manner, at least a year's supply of food, clothing, and fuel. He maintains an active system of rotation and replentishing. The tale of the ant and the grasshopper has become a favorite fireside story for his family.

f. He has become an ensign to his neighbors, rather than a recluse, and he assists them in raising their own level of existence. Though he may be viewed as intrusive by some, his overall impact will be one of progression and improvement.

g. He lives in such a way that salvage and recycling have become moral acts of thrift rather than dire necessity, and conservation has become a principle of integrity rather than a desperate concern. He cleans up his own ditch banks first.

h. He blends a creative nature and a sense of the "artist of the beautiful" with the practical acts of better water usage, necessary construciton, and other impacts on the land of his stewardship. His effort is to improve and beautify, keeping in mind, and sight, the natural scheme of things.

i. His time is the stuff from which life is made. It is managed not only to survive but to contribute to the good of all. He sees time as an ingredient for making ends meet and for "enough and to spare."

Level of Independence

However we start out, there must be established goals which carry us beyond a so-called simple life style into a more complex and mature reality of one's purpose and relationship with nature, one's fellowman, and with the universe. I use the word "complex" to illustrate one undeniable truth: man is not so simple an organism that he can be content to graze all his life. He must cultivate, water, and tend to the qualities inherent in him to become one with nature. By so doing, he understands better the principles which govern his level of independence from the unnatural. With understanding, he cannot be driven from pasture to pasture by some manipulative agent of an "escapist" philosophy.

The survival of purpose may very well determine which of us will truly inherit the earth. Meek men are not driven around, nor are they continually fleeing the rat race. What they do is provide for their own, quietly, and with a purpose.

Chapter 8

Sagebrush:
The Ancient Survival Kit

By Jim Riggs

*"For the aboriginal inhabitants of the sagebrush coun-
try ... their knowledgeable use of sagebrush afforded them
shelter, fuel, fiber, clothing, blankets, tools, medicines, and raw
material for a host of additional manufactures."*

Sagebrush first entered my consciousness when I was thirteen
years old. I stepped from the bus at Oregon Museum of Science and
Industry's Camp Hancock in the Clarno Basin of Central Oregon to find
a most extraordinary, thickly sweet aroma permeating my senses. I
didn't know then how complete and irreversible my addiction would
become, but in the years since I have learned a great deal about
sagebrush, about the rolling hills, basins, and plateaus where it grows,
about the diversity of wildlife it supports, and about the native peoples
of the sage country who considered it a most wondrous and useful
plant.

Sagebrush is the most ubiquitous shrub of the arid west. In many
areas it dominates the landscape as far as one can look in all directions. It is beauty to some and a sure sign of an uninviting wasteland
to others.

Sage grouse feed on tender young sagebrush foilage, antelope
browse on it, jack rabbits and cottontails, lizards and snakes seek shade
and protection beneath its leafy gray-green canopy and songbirds nest
in it. Farmers, ranchers, and the Bureau of Land Management battle
it with chemical sprays and massive 100-foot-plus lengths of old ships'
anchor chains dragged over the land between two bulldozers so they
can plant in its place crested wheatgrass imported from the Himalayas
for cattle fodder.

But two facts are apparaent from even a cursory look: The deli-
cate ecosystems of the sagebrush country have been drastically altered

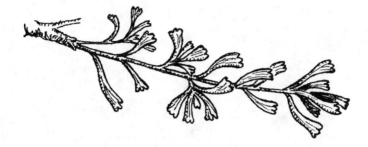

A sprig of Big Sagebrush (Artemisia tridentata) showing three-toothed leaves. (Drawing by Jim Riggs.)

by the actions of "modern" man and there is more sagebrush today than there was 150 years ago. The richer and more palatable native bunchgrasses, which had achieved a natural balance with sagebrush, had been struck a severe blow from heavy cattle and sheep overgrazing by the beginning of this century.

To the aboriginal inhabitants of the sagebrush country, and especially those of the Great Basin region of western Utah, Nevada, and southeastern Oregon, the plant was much more than a scrubby, noxious shrub that seemed to grow everywhere. Their knowledgeable use of sagebrush afforded them shelter, fuel, fiber, clothing, blankets, tools, medicines, and raw material for a host of additional manufactures. During lean times, the tiny bitter seeds even served as a rich food resource.

While approximately twenty-five species of sage have been identified in the northwest, big sage (Artemisia tridentata) is the most widespread and useful. The specific name *tridentata* describes the three-toothed leaf tips. Big sage is an extremely tenacious and prolific shrub that can reach gigantic proportions, occasionally growing fifteen feet in height, but more commonly two to four feet. In marginal habitats it may mature and reproduce at less than one foot tall. The amount of available water is the main factor determining sagebrush size, and the largest plants will be found in non-alkaline soils, along watercourses, or where the water table is deceptively close to the arid land surface.

Close-up of twining on a sagebrush bark sandal.

Preparing Sage Bark Fiber

These larger sages were sought by the native inhabitants because the gnarled trunks and limbs were thickly covered with shreddy bark that could be easily peeled off in long strips. The strongest bark is yellow to reddish-brown and lies close to the woody stems. Great quantities of this raw fiber, probably the most important resource offered by the sage, were collected and, without further refinement, used for floor covering, padding, and bedding. Sage bark provides good insulation, and an ill-prepared person lost or stranded nowadays in sagebrush country during the bitter winter cold would be wise to make use of the bark as has been done for thousands of years.

More commonly, the long strips of bark fiber were further refined by briskly rubbing them between the hands to remove the brittle, drier, outer bark. These cleaned and softened strips were then ready for the manufacture of myriad items.

Sage bark articles such as mats, blankets, and robes were manufactured solely by hand using a simple weaving technique called twining which is much easier to do than to describe. No loom is used. The body of a mat is formed by laying long bundles of bark side by side as wide as the mat is to be. These are called the "warps." The thinner bark strips, which are securely twisted around the warp bundles to hold them together, are called the "wefts."

An Oregon State University archaeological crew I worked with several years ago in a rock shelter in southeastern Oregon discovered a finely twined, perfectly preserved sage bark mat, or robe, which measured 3½ feet by 4 feet unfolded. It had been neatly folded in half twice and cached in a pit under a large flat rock at the rear of the cave. A portion of the mat later yielded a carbon-14 date of no older than 150 years.

The complete story of this mat cannot be fully reconstructed, but probably some Northern Paiute, Bannock, or Western Shoshone Indians were temporarily camped in the cave and decided not to take the mat with them when they left. They knew the cached mat would remain safe from animals and deterioration until they returned to use it again. When we excavated it, the mat seemed as fresh and pliable as the day it was made. Cached articles from other desert caves have remained in near-perfect condition for thousands of years.

Utility mats are coarsely or open-twined. The weft rows are one to several inches apart. Where more strength and solidarity are required, as for sandal soles, the rows of twining are so close they nearly conceal the warps. In one of my classes at the Malheur Field Station a student twined a full-length sage bark mat which he rolled and carried on backpacking trips. He called it his "environmental sleeping pad" and used it like the commerically produced foam pads.

Sage Bark Clothing and Footgear

In the Great Basin, animals that could provide furs and skins for clothing were scarce, so sage bark furnished a good part of the normally scant aboriginal costume. Women, and sometimes men, wore light-weight knee-length aprons—one in front and one in back—of softened, twined sage bark, or bark skirts similar to Hawaiian hula skirts. Skirts were twined for a few rows below a braided waistband, the remaining warp fibers left to hang and swish freely as a long fringe. Twined sage-bark shirts, pants, and leggins have also been recorded ethnographically, but these may be unique copies of the more recently adopted buckskin clothing and not representative of aboriginal attire.

Deep deposits in several Oregon caves have yielded highly specialized artifacts of sage-bark sandals. More than seventy-five sandals manufactured by Basin dwellers about 9,000 years ago were excavated from Fort Rock Cave in south-central Oregon in 1938 by Dr. L. S.

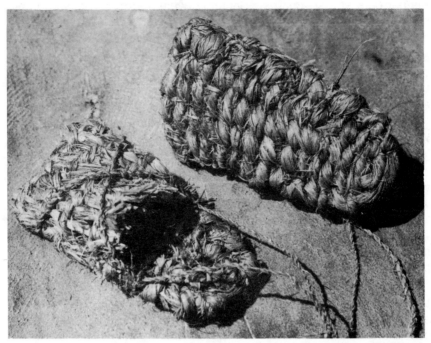

Twined sagebrush-bark sandals made by the author for the Oregon High Desert Museum. (Copy of sandal excavated from Fort Rock cave, believed to be over 9,000 years old).

Cressman of the University of Oregon. Several slight variations in style were found, but all were manufactured by close twining.

The durability of aboriginal sage-bark sandals is unknown, but modern experimentation has shown that a serviceable, although more crudely made, pair takes about three hours to make and will last through about three days of moderate wear. It is probable that sandals were worn only seasonally by the aboriginals, so they probably lasted longer.

I personally believe that sage-bark sandals were originally made to wear during winter, when snow covered the landscape, to provide welcome insulation from the cold. Worn under these conditions, sandals could last many weeks—perhaps even an entire winter. In the same region today, during milder weather, one can easily tred barefoot nine months of the year.

Several friends have twined excellently functional pairs of sandals, but perhaps their pride of manufacture has prevented them from deliberately trying to wear out their creations solely for the sake of experimental archaeology. One of these student-made sandals is now in the visitors center museum on the Hart Mountain antelope refuge as an example of aboriginal footgear.

Cordage Material

Great Basin natives literally tied their world together, and sage bark was the most commonly and frequently used fiber for cordage of all sizes. Cleaned strips were quickly twisted together with the fingers or rolled together between an open hand and the thigh to make two-ply rope. Sage bark rope is not exceptionally strong, but it is adequate for nearly all but the most specialized jobs. Stronger cord for bowstrings, animal snares, and rabbit nets was made from the finer fibers of animal sinew, stinging nettle, *Urtica*, or Indian hemp, *Apocynum*. Lacking these, people could carefully select only the strongest inner bark of sage and make do; that was the aboriginal way in sage country.

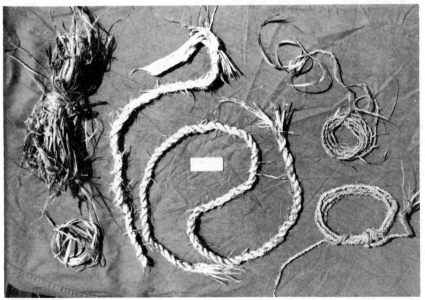

Various sizes of cordage and rope hand-twisted from sagebrush bark. Raw fiber strands shown at right.

Nature's Medicine Chest

"Doctor-brush, we call it," a Nevada Western Shoshone medicine woman said of sagebrush, for it has been and still is used in the Great Basin as an all-purpose curing plant. The old, dead, black leaves found under the bushes were powdered and placed on skin rashes, especially baby rashes. A poultice of green leaves, mashed or chewed, or a strong tea, was used to thwart bleeding of cuts, promote healing, relieve muscular bruises, aches and pains, and rheumatism and to treat gum and mouth diseases. Sage poultices on the chest and throat, and tea taken internally, relieved lung congestion and served as a general cold remedy and tonic.

Sage leaves were also chewed to relieve indigestion and gastro-intestinal disorders; as one old-time author put it, chewing the leaves "relieves the gripes and flatulence resulting from meals hastily prepared and quickly swallowed!"

When he read that sage leaves put in the nasal passages would relieve or prevent colds, a student in one of my field classes wandered about for two days with bushy sprigs of sage leaves protruding from his nostrils like a leafy green moustache. His suspected cold never materialized, so he became a believer.

One could expect a plant so materially versatile and medicinally integral to Basin cultures to have ritual significance. All sagebrush foliage was considered fortunate and formed some part of the medicine man's costume. Sage was burned at the beginning of ceremonies and it was important inside the sweat lodge where it helped to clear the sinuses, and purify the bodies and souls of the sweaters.

Among many Paiute groups, adolescent girls at their first menses were retired to small sage-covered lodges where, among other strict observances, they tied their hair with sage bark and braided circlets of bark to wear around their extremities as a guard against rheumatism. To show that they would be industrious all their lives, they also were required to gather great piles of sagebrush for firewood—obviously to the benefit of everyone in camp. If ever a Great Basin aboriginal were allergic to sagebrush, his life would be miserable indeed.

Prolific Shelter Material

As small family groups systematically harvested the sometimes abundant but widely scattered food resources of the sage country, they had little time to construct elaborate, or even semi-permanent, shelters. Camps were established wherever the food was found, but a camp among tall, thick sagebrush was preferred.

The most common temporary shelter of the Northern Paiute was constructed quickly of large sages piled up about chest-high in a circle ten or twelve feet across. Where several big sages were found growing naturally in a circle, it was easy to pile additional brush in the spaces between. A small break was left in the encirclement for a doorway and a fire was built in the center. Although the piled sage often leaned inward at the top there was no real roof.

On a solo trek through the southeastern Oregon desert one April, I found myself in the midst of a broad, sage-filled valley, darkness rapidly approaching, snow imminent and no protected caves nearby, so I hurriedly constructed an eight-foot-wide, head-high sagebrush circle in less than an hour. This type of shelter functions mainly to "break the spirit" of relentless winds. Warmth and light from my fire reflecting off the inside walls kept me comfortable in my homemade micro-environment.

One salient point I learned, however, I pass along: Don't build your fire so large that it can leap into your shelter wall, or you may find yourself inside an instantly blazing ring of fire. Fortunately, mine jumped onto a corner of the doorway and I was able to knock away that section of wall, smother the flames with dirt and rebuild with nothing damaged but my initial pride of accomplishment.

Northern Paiute circular shelter of piled sagebrush. Common temporary shelter in the Great Basin. (Drawing by Jim Riggs.)

Winter dwellings, nowadays commonly called "wickiups," were slightly more substantial. They were dome- or tepee-shaped pole frames ten to fifteen feet in diameter, sometimes thatched quickly with sagebrush, but usually made warmer amd more weatherproof with several layers of tule, cattail, or rye-grass matting.

Folk Tales of the Northern Paiutes

"Sawabe," the word for sagebrush in Northern Paiute, is a common character in many Paiute folk tales which took place back in the times when magic was commonplace and animals, plants, rocks, and people could all talk with one another. Wolf and Coyote, Isha and Itsa respectively, also lived in these times. Wolf is a good hunter, level-headed and someone to emulate, while Coyote, a clever but bungling lead character, is scatterbrained, greedy, and usually shows us graphically how not to behave. In this exerpt involving sagebrush, we learn a Paiute morality lesson.

COYOTE AND WOLF

Wolf and Coyote were brothers. Wolf was the older. They lived together in the same house. Wolf was a good hunter, he always brought back lots of game; when Coyote went hunting, he came back with nothing.

The next morning Coyote asked Wolf about rabbits. "How do you hunt them? How do you catch them so easily? You always kill many," he said to Wolf. Then his brother told him, "I pull up sagebrush and make little piles. Then I look back and they are all rabbits."

So this Coyote wanted to hunt the same way as his brother. He wanted to see how well he could do it. He found sagebrush. He piled it high as he went along, then he looked back and the piles all turned into rabbits. He said, "That's an easy way to hunt. I have plenty. I'll have to eat these right now, I can bring the next ones home." Then he ate all those rabbits.

He went to another place and piled more sagebrush and went off a little distance and looked back, and there they were—nothing but piles of sagebrush. There were no rabbits. He had spoiled it. He brought nothing home that night and that's how Coyote spoiled easy hunting.

The Great Basin Dweller

In terms of survival ease, the American Great Basin is one of the least lucrative regions for habitation. Yet, as tenacious and adaptable as the sagebrush on which they relied, Basin peoples applied their cumulative cultural knowledge and flourished for more than 10,000 years. These people respected their environment, learned to use without selfish exploitation, manipulate without attempted subjugation, and experienced fulfilling lives.

Peoples of dissimilar cultural backgrounds may view the same scene, yet perceive it entirely differently. Maybe the next time you visit sagebrush country you will see something you missed before. Maybe you'll tangle with sagebrush and Coyote out there. I have, and they won.

Peoples in the Klamath area made sandals and moccasin-like boots of tules (Scirpis), but a Northern Paiute woman from Surprise Valley, in northeastern California, commented, "Tules are no good for shoes. Sagebrush is nice and warm even if it gets wet."

Roots, seeds, berries, and meat were sun-dried for winter use and were stored in large, twined sage bark bags buried in dry protected

Coiled sagebrush basket made by Aynne Brinitzer in a Malhuer Field Station course conducted by the author.

places until needed. This caching of foods and material items was a common trait of Basin peoples who, in their seasonal rounds of food collecting, traveled frequently and extensively and could not be encumbered with less-than-vital possessions. They were, however, masters at improvising tools and articles they needed on the spot, using whatever raw materials were at hand. Many items were quickly manufactured for a specific purpose, used, then discarded. New articles were again made when the need arose, and previously cached materials were found and re-used. So, instead of carrying the weight of their worldly possessions on their backs, they simply carried the necessary knowledge in their heads and applied it when called for. Handy!

Fire-Making Materials and Techniques

Fire was precious and necessary in the lives of Basin aborigines, and sagebrush was most integral to the making and maintaining of fire. Only the hand-twirled drill was used to create fire. As the drill was twirled rapidly in a socket of the hearth piece, the friction ground off blackened wood powder. Increased speed and pressure created smoke and eventually (with luck and the blessing of the Great Spirit), a live coal formed in the collected powder. Twirling stopped, the coal was lightly tapped into a waiting wad of tinder and gently blown with short

Great Basin style fire drill and hearth of sagebrush wood.

"Slow match" or sagebrush fire bundle.

puffs until it burst into flame. Very dry, finely shredded sage bark was preferred then and still makes the best tender I have used. The hearth and drill were often fashioned from dead "punky" sage wood. Because long, straight, sage branches are scarce, a short piece of sage would frequently be used for the drill. Carried in a waterproof pouch, it would be tied onto any longer straight stick found at the campsite.

Even for the experienced, making fire this way was not a certainty, especially in damp weather, so fires were maintained as long as possible. Fire was often transported from one camp to another via the fire bundle or "slow match." Naturally, the fire bundle was also made of sage bark.

The one-to-two-foot-long bundle was constructed in layers and bound together with more bark strips. In cross-section it would have unrefined bark outside, lightly shredded bark inside that, and a center core of very finely shredded "fuzzed-up" bark. When they broke camp, the Indians spread open one end of the bundle to expose the fine inner core, shoved in a live, marble-sized coal and blew on it lightly. Once smoldering, the inner core kept the coal alive while the coarser outer layers kept it from burning through the bundle too rapidly. A well-made fire bundle would smolder flamelessly for ten to fifteen hours before it burned too short to carry conveniently. If the travelers had not reached their destination by this time, they would stop, kindle a new fire by blowing the remainder of the bundle into flame, then manufacture a new bundle and carry on.

Sagebrush makes excellent firewood. Although it burns fast, it gives off terrific light and heat, and wet or green sage ignites almost as readily as dry dead branches. It is a very special feeling to bask in the glow of a sage fire in the vastness of the desert.

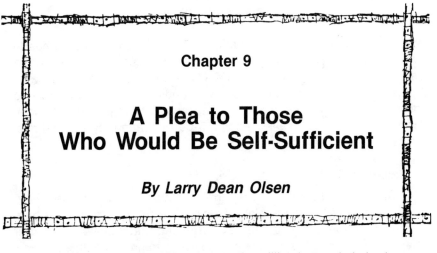

Chapter 9

A Plea to Those
Who Would Be Self-Sufficient

By Larry Dean Olsen

*"The freedom granted by nature to the willing learner is indeed
pleasant. To simply stay in that condition, however, would
be as limiting as having been born and
locked into a stone-age condition."*

Self-sufficiency in its most desirable context is to build toward a condition of life whereby a family, or individuals, may be independent and self-sustaining within their own social environment by producing much of what they consume.

For most Americans this would mean freedom from debt; it would also mean a degree of freedom from conditions causing them to be more or less dependent upon someone, or something outside their control.

For example, a man who wants a warm blanket for his bed may get it in a number of ways. If he is totally dependent upon society for his need, the blanket may come to him via welfare. If he is only partly dependent upon society for the blanket, he may buy it with money he has earned. If he is even less dependent on the market place, with its changing trends, shortages, and inflationary uncertainties, he may get a blanket through his own ingenuity in salvaging, recycling, advance planning, buying items on special, or by a cooperative effort with his family and friends which may bring together the necessary products to make a blanket or quilt.

If he is independent of all these conditions, he would have a blanket only if he made it himself, from scratch. This would mean wool sheared from his own sheep, carded, spun, and woven on instruments of his own making.

It seems simple enough to have defined self-sufficiency with such an example, but building toward the best self-sufficiency requires some additional philosophy and definitions. First of all, it would be nearly impossible for a person to provide all of his present-day needs and to be totally independent all of his life. There isn't any virtue in it anyway. Self-sufficiency can be broadened by extending one's independence to include the family. Then it might be necessary to form another social group which could be called a band, tribe, or community. Beyond this, self-sufficiency may become fuzzy.

A Mature Outlook

Another broadening of the term "self-sufficiency" is a definition of a standard of life. If we think of a simple lean-to or shack, or a bare sustenance level of living, our self-sufficient status may be no better than that of a dependent welfare recipient. A hand-to-mouth existence, even when produced every whit from scratch, is still poverty. Some definitions of self-sufficiency today are as poor as the people who try to live them. Self-sufficiency involves a mature outlook on life's goals and makes provisions for service to others.

A system of progression, and the production of surplus, gives meaning to self-sufficient living. It provides a blueprint for the future whereby increase and example set standards for the world. When a people are enslaved to the masters of debt, and the unbending consequences of economic evil and designs, truly self-sufficient and independent working groups of people will become an ensign to nations simply because they will know how to produce for themselves a high standard of life. They will possess a certain pride in workmanship and design; they will promote an environment of individual freedom from want and outside control. The moral level of the community will be high and coopertive effort will be the principle method of production, with free enterprise as the method of distribution. Individual efforts will be honored within the framework of the community where free expression and direction of effort will be held inviolate.

An Honorable Experience

Since a cooperative and organized effort has always produced more under a free enterprise system than has any other system, we are brought to the realization that a total, independent "aloneness" self-sufficiency is less desirable even if it is attractive. However, the *ability* to take care of one's self *is* a desirable goal. This comes only with exposure and practice. Hence, many go to the deserts or the mountains to become one with the realities of nature, to exist in a primal abundance of wild foods, shelters, and challenges. The freedom granted by nature to the willing learner is indeed pleasant. To simply stay in that conditon, however, would be as limiting as having been born and locked into a stone-age condition.

Because we may choose today a life style from almost any example of the past, on through what is today's grandest imagination, an experience in total self-sufficiency is honorable only as long as it is but a part of the whole of life.

Therefore, learning to live off the land, to support oneself in a pristine environment, is a worthy goal and perhaps fundamental to the well-being of any person today. Once mastered, the charge to prepare every needful thing and to become independent over all things is fulfilled. From then on you are perfected in that realm of existence and the fear of want doesn't exist anymore. Then it is time to lead out in other essentials like family, community, and the excellence of honest, life-serving progress both in technology and social morality.

Chapter 10

Bulrush Weaving

By Linda Jamison

*"Value comes from experience and the amount of yourself that
is invested in a particular project. The more difficult . . . the
more valuable the finished piece."*

I've been going into the field with my husband in various capacities since 1973; first as a student, then as an assistant instructor and finally as an instructor. Because of my particular interest in plants it was a natural evolution for me to begin teaching basketry on the trips. Our students seem to enjoy learning weaving techniques and it adds to the total experience. And you get a feeling of satisfaction when you are able to collect your own materials from the surrounding habitat and make something useful from start to finish—totally.

We needed containers for gathering berries and other items, so our first project was a pouch made from cattail leaves. It was a learning experience. We used fresh cattail leaves, and the finished bags looked great. But the next morning was a revelation. During the night the leaves had shrunk so much that our containers looked more like fish nets. Thus we learned that to eliminate shrinking the materials had to dry, then be dampened again for flexibility. Subsequent projects were much improved.

My appetite for learning whetted, I began to search for better-suited, stronger fibers. I found that yucca leaves were much more durable than cattail leaves, but they take a lot of time to prepare and they weren't always available in places where we conducted our trips. Since then I have learned that bulrush is reasonably durable, easy to gather, easy to prepare, and nearly always available for weaving material. They work up fast so finished baskets, mats, sandals, and other projects can be completed during the trip.

A large variety of mats, baskets and bowls can be woven from bulrush and other similar plant leaves using a combination of plaited and twined weaves.

Most Indian baskets are twined, or coiled, and made from sumac, willow, or yucca fibers or stems. Bulrush is not as durable as these materials, of course, but one can learn the techniques of weaving and eventually expand the process into more lasting projects. You can't do that with sumac or willow because the splitting, peeling, and stripping technique takes considerable time as well as talent to master.

I find it interesting that most Indians believe weaving to be "woman's work," but I have noticed that men enjoy basketry and weaving almost as much as women do. My husband, Richard, and I went to the Ute reservation to learn the coiling technique from an Indian weaver (it's something you almost have to see to learn). Po Chief Mike, the old woman who demonstrated the method for us, laughed when she learned that Richard was just as interested in learning the method as I was.

Materials

I believe that using natural materials for baskets and other weavings adds a unique element to the finished project. After the introductory lecture of my "city" course, we go on a field trip to gather materials. This is often the first real awareness many people have that these are *really* natural materials, in the truest sense of the word.

Value comes from experience and from the amount of yourself you invest in a particular project. The more difficult or traumatic or worthy the experience, the more valuable the finished piece. I suppose that is the reason I don't sell my work; I doubt that anyone would offer me an equitable price, nor would they be able to understand that each piece has a certain amount of myself in it: none are perfect, but they are all valuable.

An important part of rushcraft is in the selecting and preparing of the materials. Rushes most commonly used for weaving are *Scirpus lacustris*. In Europe, they can apparently be purchased in bolts. However, I've looked for bulrush in stores and I haven't been able to find it in the United States. Thus you are reduced to collecting your own and storing it for off-season use. Any species of Scirpus will do.

Harvesting should be done in the summer or fall before rust spots begin to appear, and you'll want to gather a variety of sizes for different projects. I like to use large-diameter rushes for large mats and to add design to smaller pieces. You can create interesting patterns with last year's discolored rushes. Now that I've worked with bulrush for a number of years I naturally know what to look for when I am gathering my materials. You will know, too.

The harvesting experience, particularly if there are difficulties associated with it, makes each finished basket more valuable to its creator.

On one such rainy-day field trip, a student came face to face with a *very* large spider whose web was strung between two perfect specimens of bulrush. The spider was left undisturbed, of course, but the student's project reflected the experience: it was a large, circular wall hanging. The ends were left unfinished to resemble the eight-legged arachnid.

Another student's dog literally ate a portion of his almost-completed basket. Needless to say he was infuriated . . . considering the effort that had gone into it, but with a little help he was able to replace the damaged weavers. The basket now sits (out of canine reach) on a shelf as a reminder of the experience.

I mention this incident so you will know that, as a medium, bulrushes are quite forgiving. Damaged or broken leaves can be replaced after the fact, and it is easy to just "tuck in" wayward pieces.

The best way to prepare rushes or cattail leaves is to spread them out in a shady spot and turn them occasionally for even drying. Freshly cut leaves can be used when they reach the proper stage and while they are still pliable, or they can be thoroughly dried for storage and later use. Once dried they must be "rehydrated." Sprinkle them with water and wrap in a damp cloth to keep them flexible as you work. Avoid getting the leaves waterlogged. This causes them to shrink. Eventually you will recognize the "spongy" feel of properly prepared rushes—if they are too fresh or too dry they will "crack" when squeezed.

I suppose that the only real disadvantage to using bulrush for weaving is that it generally takes several hours to reconstitute the rushes properly, so it isn't a hobby you can decide to do at the spur of the moment with your materials immediately at hand, the way you can with bead-work or knitting.

Reconstituting rushes is often a problem when I teach classes in rushcraft. My students forget to prepare their materials the evening before and they come with hastily dampened rushes. The finished projects are almost a waste of their time because the leaves break and crack as they are bent.

Technique

Most rush weaving can be done without tools. Plaited and twined weaves are well-suited to finger weaving. However, some people like to use an awl and scissors and a sailmaker's needle. At home I use an awl, scissors, and forceps to help pull loose ends through the weave and to finish off the edges. In the field I find that a knife is all I need. I also like to keep a damp rag handy to wipe each rush as I use it. This helps keep it pliable as I work.

Selection of rushes is important. They should be of matching thickness and they should be sound—discard any spotty or rusted ones. An exception would be when you use spotted or dark-colored rushes for effect and design—for that you should select the best quality you can find.

For small mats and basic baskets you may use the plaited, or checked, weave (one under and one over). Begin with ten matched rushes that have been flattened between the fingers until they are as thin as possible.

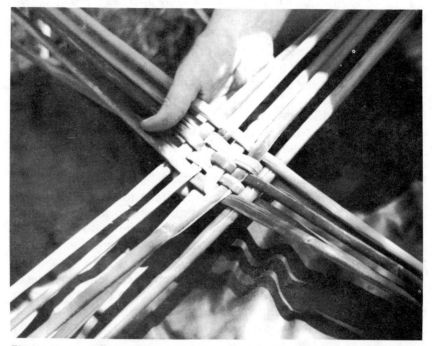

Flatten the rushes and begin with an easy plaited (over one under one) weave for the base of your basket or mat.

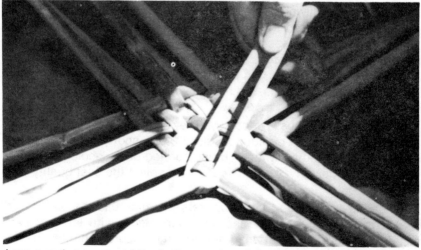

Loop a rush over one of the bottom corner stakes making a pair of weavers.

Once you have plaited the first ten rushes by the "over one, under one" method, begin the twined weave. To start, bend a rush in half and loop it behind the first stake (the base rushes are called "stakes," the rush being used is called the "weaver"), making a pair of weavers we will call "A" and "B." Pass weaver "A" over "B" in front of the first stake and behind the second stake as shown in figure 1. (I promise it is really

Twine around the base, being sure to pull the weave tight in order to "damp" the plaited weave together.

not as difficult to do as it is to explain.) Then pass weaver "B" over "A" in front of the second stake and behind the third stake, as in figure 2. Continue, using the weavers alternately until two rounds are completed. Pull the twined weave tight to secure the plaited base weave.

When the weavers become short, add another rush by laying the smallest end of the new piece on top of the short weaver and work double for two or three strokes. As you weave, move the stakes until they are evenly spaced (they will work themselves into a circle). If you want a deep basket, you should begin to shape the sides upward by pulling the twined weave more tightly after a couple of rounds. Of course, if you are making a mat, continue to weave flat.

Once your piece is the desired size, finish it by threading the weavers down through four rounds of weave, then draw each stake down through four rounds of twining (see figure 3). Continue to do this until all ends are finished. If you have an awl and sailmaker's needle this job will be much easier. Work the awl up through the four rounds of

Make several rounds of twining, then add additional stakes on the corners. This mat began with ten stakes. Now there are fourteen.

twining to open it slightly. Push the needle into this opening, thread the rush through the eye of the needle and pull it down through the rounds of weaving. Cut the ends off so they don't show.

Another method of starting a basket or mat is called the "spider" base. It is begun by tying seven rushes tightly together in the middle and bending the stakes over the string, like hairpins, to give fourteen radials in proper order. Then, with a fine, pliable weaver, work a twined weave for about one inch, then add more stakes as shown in figure 4. After every inch of twining add more stakes to keep the twined weave close.

To add a handle, just braid a section of rush leaving both ends loose about six inches longer than the handle. Pull it through the top round of the basket before it is finished so that the finish damping will tie it securely into the basket.

You will undoubtedly come up with your own innovations when you work in this medium. Bulrushes lend themselves well to experimentation.

A small willow was wrapped with the end stakes to strengthen the top of this basket. An awl is used to lift the twined rows to insert the ends and make them less conspicuous.

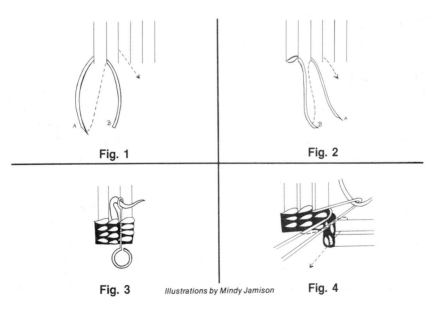

Fig. 1   Fig. 2

Fig. 3   *Illustrations by Mindy Jamison*   Fig. 4

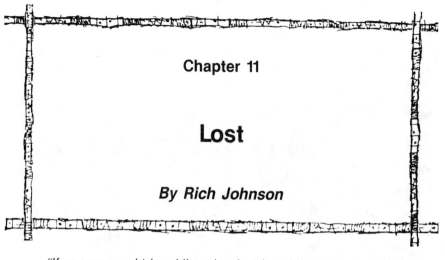

Chapter 11

Lost

By Rich Johnson

"If you are caught in a blizzard or lost in cold weather, don't be afraid to sleep. Pinching and punching yourself to stay awake uses up energy that your body needs to create warmth."

You've laughed at the old-timer who would never admit to being lost—"Jest a bit bum-fuzzled 'bout my whereabouts," but this state of temporary confusion can be, and often is, a terrifying experience. Nevertheless, some meditation and training in clear thinking and direction-finding can spare you an uncomfortable, anxious night in the open.

Procedure To Follow When Lost

1. Sit down, relax, think through your situation and make a plan of action. Decide whether to stay where you are, and wait, or to go on. Some factors to consider in making that decision include whether or not the area has a water supply. Whether it is dangerous to remain (on a cliff, near raging water etc.), whether there is enough shelter material, if weather conditions warrant protection from the elements, and whether or not you will be missed in the area where you became lost.

2. If you decide to stay put for the night, build a fire and a windbreak, and gather bedding.

3. If you decide to continue on, mark your origination point in some conspicious manner. Keep your base camp in view and use it as a hub. Make a large circle, observing the area for a trail or signs of travel. If you find none, you must then decide on your direction of travel. If you have a compass, set your course on a sighted landmark; if you have no compass, pick a landmark and hike to it. Stay with this course until you find a trail or a road which will lead to civilization. There are very

few places left in the United States where you can hike indefinately without reaching a road or some type of civilization, unless you are going in circles, and people who are lost often do.

Signals

If you have the means, or the knowledge, to get a fire going remember that dense smoke by day or bright fire by night may attract the attention of searchers or Forest Service employees who are on the lookout for fires. Care must be taken to clear the ground where the fire will be started to prevent starting a serious forest or grass fire. Green growth such as grass, ferns, and live brush will make a heavy smoke, but add this fuel to the fire carefully so you won't put it out.

If you see or hear a plane, get into as open an area as possible; it may be part of a search party. Try to signal with clothing or other bright material. Obviously, shouting will do no good.

Firing a gun to summon help is not likely to get results in the daytime during hunting season. At night, however, gunfire means trouble or illegal hunting, either of which may bring help. Don't waste ammunition, though. Fire three shots in succession about three to five minutes apart, then listen for answering shots. If your shot is answered fire again; if not, save your ammunition and try again the next night.

What To Do At Night

Begin preparation early. Essentials are: (a) plenty of dry firewood to last the night, (b) a good supply of kindling to bring the fire up fast if it begins to die down, and (c) a windbreak which will reflect the heat of your fire. A boulder, a cut bank, or a snowbank with brush piled against it, or crossed poles strung between two trees and thatched with boughs or brush, will serve as your windbreak reflector. Cover the ground area where your bed will be with dry pine needles, dry leaves or boughs for insulation and be sure the bed is far enough from the fire to avoid having it catch on fire from sparks.

If the night is cold, sleeping between two fires will help keep you warm. Use common sense and don't build the fires too close together. Sparks or flame might set your clothes or hair on fire. But don't build them so far apart that you lose the benefit from warm air circulating between and above the fires. You will probably awaken several times during the night to replentish your fire, but don't try to stay awake to feed it or build it up too large to avoid getting up in the night. And don't worry about falling asleep in the cold; sleep and rest are the best possible remedies in an emergency situation. If you become too uncomfortable, you will wake up.

Vilhjalmur Stevansson in his book "Artic Manual" has this to say about going to sleep in cold weather:

> "One of the hardest of false beliefs to eradicate is, 'when lost in a blizzard you must keep moving, you must not go to sleep, for if you do you will never wake again.'
>
> "The principles to remember are: Don't keep moving—keep still. Keep your clothes dry. Sleep as much as you can, because it both saves energy and passes time."

So if you are caught in a blizzard or lost in cold weather, don't be afraid to sleep. Pinching and punching yourself to stay awake uses up energy your body needs to create warmth. Panic and exercise activate your sweat glands and perspiration will make your clothing wet. Then when you are so worn out that you cannot keep awake any longer, exhausted and wet, you drop in your tracks—*then* you may never wake again.

The following quote is from James Rogers, Chairman of the Camping and Activities Committee, Adirondack Council of the Boy Scouts.

> "There is one phase of being lost that is seldom mentioned as far as I know, that is going up a mountain. Almost everyone hiking in mountain country hikes for the purpose of reaching the top of some peak. This is usually a well-defined trail to the top, but the top itself is bare. As a result, when the person starts down the mountain, he or she misses the trail and continues on down in the dense growth.
>
> "By following . . . a stream to the nearest house, etc., they get into considerable trouble. For some reason, they never seem to have sense enough to turn around and go back to the top of the mountain.
>
> "Search parties usually look on the tops of mountains for missing persons, if they return to the top they will probably be found. Even if they are not found their chances of picking up a forest road or trail is greater at the top."

The advice to "follow a stream" often comes without thinking, even from seasoned outdoorsmen. Don't forget that—while springs feed brooks and go on to eventually become rivers—springs, brooks and rivers also feed lakes which cannot be crossed and may take many hours to circle.

There is much evidence on the relation of faith to the maintenance of courage and the control of fear, particularly in situations where people are lost. Five-year-old Pamela Hollingsworth was found after eight days on Mt. Chocorua in New Hampshire in October. Her parents said that she express her complete faith in "Father, Mother and God."

Perhaps it is such faith and courage that brings many lost young-sters out alive while many grownups lose heart, quit, and die.

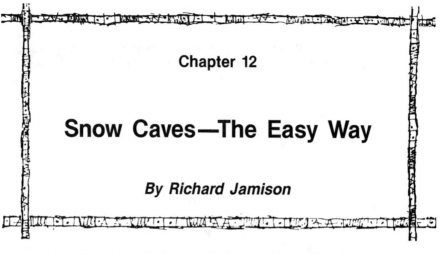

Chapter 12

Snow Caves—The Easy Way

By Richard Jamison

*"... it remained between thirty-two and thirty-eight degrees
inside our snow cave, although the temperature outside
was well below zero and the wind was blowing."*

More people than ever are finding the snow provides pleasure and a welcome escape from the frustration of being cooped up all winter in an office or some other confining job. Snowshoeing, ice fishing, cross-country skiing and snowmobiling are becoming increasingly popular.

Cross-country skiers and snowmobilers can put quite a few miles between themselves and their starting point in just a couple of hours. If an emergency arises (and I have seen storms come in so fast that all signs of landmarks and tracks are erased), the difficulty in getting back increases with each mile. Sadly, two young men on snowmobiles died near my home just last winter. They lacked winter survival knowledge and were not prepared to meet the emergency.

When you plan winter outings give some thought to your clothing. Check your equipment, map out your route, get a weather report. Give yourself an edge. Then, if you do get in trouble, remember to keep your head. Analyze the situation. Utilize all the know-how you have.

In my estimation, snowmobilers carry too little gear in case of emergencies. It is true that I usually espouse "let nature provide," but winter survival is a new game.

I strongly recommend that winter sportsmen carry as much of the following gear as is reasonable for their mode of travel: a shovel (the small army collapsible models are nice and sturdy), a machette or sheath knife, fire starter, sleeping bag, poncho or plastic bags, candle and emergency rations, and a small metal cup for melting snow over a fire.

Snow storms can move in quickly and erase all signs of trails and landmarks.

For survival, your first consideration will be how to keep dry and warm. I can't stress too strongly that *dry means warm.*

Snow can be your greatest asset. Snow is one of nature's best insulators, and a snow cave will help you conserve valuable body heat by getting you out of the wind chill.

The old method of digging snow caves started with a small opening, enlarged through an entrance hole until it was large enough to sleep in. My exerience with this method was negative; I always wound up with wet clothes and a backache so I had never been much of a winter camping advocate until a few years ago.

I was discussing this very problem with a friend and he told me that he had developed a method that eliminated the stooping and effort of digging a snow cave.

Ernest Wilkinson is a taxidermist and trapper by trade. He conducts backpacking trips in the summer and snow trips in the winter near Monte Vista, Colorado. As an avocation he raises mountain lions, badgers, wolves, coyotes and other animals which he films for national television and movies. Needless to say Ernie is not an armchair survivalist; he has spent most of his life in the wilderness, and I am always open to techniques that make a difficult task easier and to learning new survival methods to pass along to my students. So when Ernie suggested that we take a week-end trip to try out his method of snow cave construction I jumped at the chance.

Winter Campsite

We took snowmobiles to an area about five miles past Ground Hog Park in the San Luis Mountains and carefully chose our campsite. Winter campsite selection is very important because of potential avalanche danger. Every year winter travelers lose their lives to hat-hanging snow that breaks loose high above on the ridges, causing tons of snow to rush down.

The "condition" of the snow should be considered when you choose your campsite. Windblown drifts that have crusted over are good for digging a snow cave. Powder snow is not because it won't hold together. We chose a large, wind-blown drift about a hundred feet from a stand of trees and built a fire to melt snow for drinking and to warm ourselves during the construction process. Remember to locate your shelter close enough to firewood so valuable energy is not wasted in hauling wood.

A novice will take about two hours to complete a snow cave, so if you are a novice start preparations early. You won't want to be caught still digging after dark.

In ideal conditions the snow will be crusty and solid throughout the drift. It can be taken out of the cave in blocks or large chunks. A machete is best for this work, but shovels or a snowshoe also work well.

Hat-hanging snow on high mountain tops poses a threat to outdoor enthusiasts.

Winter expert, Ernest Wilkinson, displays the various types of tools that should be carried by snowmobilers in case of emergencies.

In an emergency you may have to use your hands to dig through the snow, or you can use a piece of wood with a flattened edge.

Ernie and I began by digging a large entrance about four feet wide and four feet high (see diagram). It could have been larger, depending on the size of the snow drift and the size of the shelter we planned to construct. There is no need to build a four-man shelter if there are only two people in your party. The larger the cavity, the larger the space to heat, and the fewer bodies there are to supply body heat the colder you will be. If there are more than five people in your group, and if there is time, it is best to divide into two groups and dig two caves.

If you have chosen a drift large enough (as we did), you can begin by digging high so that the snow can be "rolled" out with little effort. I don't mean that you should build on a steep incline, because you will want to recover some of the snow from the cavity to fill the entrance.

The job will go much faster with team-work. Ernie and I used a system where one of us, inside, pushed the snow out and the other cleared the entrance. The hole was big enough to stand in, so we eliminated a lot of stooping, crawling, and getting wet in the snow.

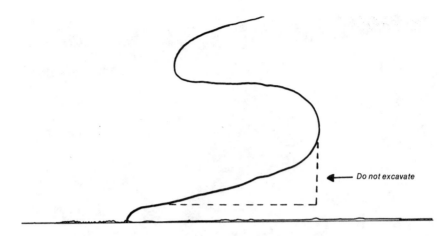

Fig. 1. *Dig uphill, slope the back of the cave slightly. Do not excavate the floor at the back of the cave.*

Once a cavity is completed, the roof can be shaped into a dome; take care not to break through the ceiling. A rounded dome gives strength to the ceiling and traps warm air in the upper part of the shelter.

Forming A Bench

Next we used snow from the ceiling to form benches. The formation of these benches, and their placement in the shelter, is most important if you want to stay warm. If they are too low you will be sleeping in a cold air draft. The benches should be parallel with the opening and separated by a trench (see diagram). Cold air flows through the entrance and along the trench while warm air from your body heat is trapped in the dome (see diagram). After the benches were leveled we allowed them to "set up" for about twenty minutes before moving our gear inside.

The old method called for the gear to be taken in through a small entrance and it became covered with snow during the process. If you tried to take large items like a packsack into the snow cave the entrance had to be widened, then repaired. The ensuing struggle wasted energy that could have been saved for more necessary work.

We laid our ponchos on the benches, then our foam pads and we finally rolled out our sleeping bags. This layer of insulation is important. Seventy percent of body heat escapes downward. Snow can melt beneath you and cause you to be quite uncomfortable. (Remember, dry means warm.) Pine boughs make good insulation. Pine needles can

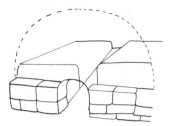

Fig. 2. *Leave a trench between the benches. The height of the benches is important to keep the sleeper above the cold air flow.*

Fig. 3. *When properly constructed, the warm air will be trapped in the dome and the cold air will circulate through the trench and opening.*

When the excavation is completed the sleeping gear is moved in and placed on the benches. The wide entrance gives greater ease in moving about.

be used where snow isn't too deep to find them. They make good insulation in an emergency.

With all of the gear inside, we closed the large entrance hole from outside the shelter with blocks of snow which we had removed from inside the cavity. We packed loose snow into all the cracks.

While we waited for the snow to "set up" (about twenty minutes), we warmed ourselves by the fire and drank water from snow we had melted. The body uses an amazing amount of moisture during winter activities that must be replaced to prevent dehydration. You can determine whether or not you are getting enough water by the color of your urine, if it is dark yellow you had better take time to drink plenty of liquids, whether you feel thirsty or not.

The entrance is closed with blocks of snow that was removed from the cave and then cave entrance opened at bottom of wall.

After the snow crusted we cut a small opening at the bottom of the entrance wall. The secret to staying warm in a snow shelter is to sleep higher than the entrance hole, so we were careful to dig the opening low.

Our cave was finished in record time, the gear was inside with no effort, my back didn't ache and I wasn't even wet. Ernie's method worked beautifully, but then he had spent years perfecting it and I appreciated the time he spent sharing his skill with me.

That night we slept comfortably. In our snow cave the temperature was thirty-two to thirty-eight degrees. The outside temperature was well below zero and the wind was blowing.

Fire Not Necessary

Many people have the misconception that it is necessary to build a fire to keep warm. Actually a fire inside a snow cave causes the snow to glaze and prevents it from "breathing" much like a nylon tent breathes. Moisture trapped inside actually causes dampness which can be uncomfortable and cold at best, and dangerous at worst. There is always the possibility that your entrance could snow over cutting off your air flow. In that case a fire can burn up your oxygen in a very short time, and you will suffocate.

I believe this is the best and fastest method of snow cave construction for one person or for a group. Just remember to take the necessary precautions for a safe trip, and plan a special "snow cave expedition" sometime during the winter. You will be surprised at how comfortable you can be, and it is best to have experienced a skill before it becomes a necessity.

As we left the San Luis Valley I contemplated the irony of our trip. Our shelters had been constructed at the location where General Fremont and his party had experienced a fateful winter many years ago in their search for a pass through the mountain range. I wondered if they took advantage of the insulation properties of snow as we had.

Ernest and Gary Doolittle relax in the comfort of the completed snow cave, oblivious to the outside weather.

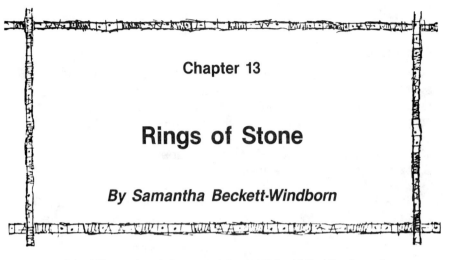

Chapter 13

Rings of Stone

By Samantha Beckett-Windborn

". . . skills we teach borrowed from original inhabitants. . . ."

"Survivalist" is a word that has been adopted by a number of groups with diverse philosophies to describe themselves and their organizations.

Like bomb shelters in the 1950s, "survivalism" is a sign of the times and of the uncertainty most of us feel in light of the economy and the course of politics. The result is that many are doing something about becoming more self-sufficient and preparing for an event of emergency wherein they would have only themselves to rely on for the necessities of life.

Lately I have noticed three basic philosophies: the *coffee can* survivalists whom I see as backpackers who take a "kit" everywhere they go; the *sewer* survivalists who take a stash of canned goods and an arsenal that would be the envy of the IRA and hole up in some underground or secluded spot and wait for their hungry neighbors to come begging (and subsequently be blown to a better world); and the third group I've come to think of as *Abo's* (for Aboriginal life style).

I consider myself akin to the third group. The skills we teach were borrowed from the original inhabitants of this and other continents. It is their technology and the skills they developed for living *with* (not necessarily "off") the land which we have "re-learned."

As an anthropologist, historian, and student of native American history, I have come to love those people, and to realize how great their influence was on the history of all of us—and on the whole world.

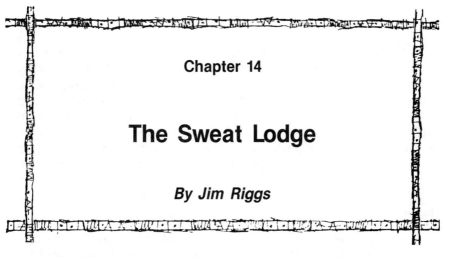

Chapter 14

The Sweat Lodge

By Jim Riggs

"We three were initiating the new lodge with what would be the hottest series of sweats I have ever taken . . . perhaps ever hope to take!"

When the fire had burned to a great heap of glowing coals and hot rocks, Lem said we were ready. He dunked himself in the pond, grabbed the bucket of water warming by the fire and entered the sweat lodge; a waist-high, five-foot-wide willow-dome heavily covered with blankets, sleeping bags, and canvas.

Michael and I rolled the glowing rocks—the heavy porous ones Lem had collected—from the fire and with sharply bent green-willow tongs carried them to the lodge. Just inside the lodge, to the left of the doorway, we had dug an eighteen-inch-wide and deep pit and lined it with thin, flat slabs of rock.

Lem sat inside and, with two short sticks, arranged the rocks in the pit, carefully removing any adhering live coals that might make the lodge smoky. When the pit was full Michael and I waded into the pond, submerged our heads to thoroughly wet our hair, then stooped to back into the lodge.

Lem is a hereditary chief of the Nez Perce tribe from Lapwai, Idaho, who was taking my spring course at Eastern Oregon State College. Michael had selected this spot and built the sweat lodge as a class project. We three were initiating the new lodge with what would be the hottest series of sweats I have ever taken . . . perhaps ever hope to take.

Intense heat met us at the doorway. Lem had already sprinkled water onto the rocks to "warm the lodge up," he said. We settled ourselves comfortably, straight-backed, cross-legged on the burlap flooring and sat for a few minutes adjusting to the heat, breathing deeply through our noses.

Michael dropped the door blanket then tucked it snugly at sides and bottom so no slivers of light could be seen. The lodge was totally dark except for the vibrantly glowing pit of rocks. The temperature increased. I crumbled some dried sweetgrass (Heirochloe odorata) and sprinkled it over the rocks. Bits of grass instantly became tiny, unseen puffs of sweet and thick aromatic smoke which we inhaled. Lem dashed a sagebrush frond of water across the rocks. A hissing wall of steam rose along the curvature of the lodge and began to condense, then settled down and began to engulf us.

Intense Heat

As we talked quietly in our isolated lodge in northestern Oregon's Wallowa Mountains, massive blue-black thunderheads were shifting, building overhead. A pileated woodpecker cackled from high in the forest canopy. Lem slowly but steadily increased the heat; as each new wave leveled and our bodies adjusted, he sprinkled on more water. Our pores opened widely. Perspiration and condensation streamed down our bodies. We were careful not to breathe on each other because the sensation is akin to being on fire.

Without warning the sky rumbled as if awakening from some long and disoriented sleep. Thunder suddenly, wildly crashed around our tiny black hemisphere of open pores and minds. In my recollection, the ground vibrated and the lodge shook.

"It is a good day for a sweat," Lem responded with another dash of water. "I think Chief Joseph is smiling on us."

We smiled back. *Hin-mah-too-yah-lat-kekht*, the real name of the venerable Nez Perce chief whose ancestral home was the Wallowa Valley, translates to English as "Thunder Traveling to Loftier Mountain Heights."

Taxing our limits, we endured a last sprinkle of water, gave a whoop in unison, and crawled from the darkness into the outside world. Light. Water. Michael and I streaked into the pond; Lem, dripping and dignified, just moseyed toward the water and sat on a rock for a few minutes before slowly immersing himself.

The entire experience of constructing the lodge and the ritual of the first sweat had built up to this singular moment of total mental-physical sensation. There was no shock upon diving into the cold mountain water, only an elusively pleasurable sensation adequately described by Reginald Laubin in "The Indian Tipi" as feeling "like an angel, with no bones, and about to fly away."

There was no shock upon diving into the cold mountain water, only an elusively pleasurable sensation adequately described by Reginald Laubin in "The Indian Tipi" as feeling "like an angel, with no bones, and about to fly away."

After a few moments (or eons?) of floating weightlessly, allowing the electrically rippling water to wash away the sweat and bodily grime, we drank heartily, waded out carefully (equilibrium plays tricks) and silently perched on large boulders, gazing. We felt clean, refreshed, alert and harmoniously receptivie to all things spiritual and natural, all things good. The edges of our surroundings—trees, rocks, mountains, clouds and each other—were gilded with a peculiar light from an unknown source: all seemed to move, not to somewhere else, but in place, from within. And these are only the describable sensations.

Three more times that day we re-entered the sweat lodge. Each round surpassed the one before, until daylight waned, the rocks cooled, and we returned to the everyday world.

Lodge Types Vary

Sweating was integral for nearly all native groups in aboriginal North America, although the form, size, and building materials of the lodge, the symbolism and ritual procedures of the sweat, varied considerably with environmental and cultural factors. Sweat houses could be permanent, underground rooms, semi-subterranean structures covered with poles, boughs and dirt, low split-plank buildings, clay- or adobe-covered domes resembling Pueblo ovens, or the most ubiquitous—the willow-frame dome covered with mats and skins (later, blankets and canvas) described here.

For the Nez Perce, and probably for other native peoples, sweating had any one of three purposes: (1) physical and spiritual cleansing and conditioning; (2) curing; and (3) recreation. Besides the documented healthful effects (see Mikkel Aaland's excellent book "Sweat" published by Capra Press), native sweating contributed to an individual's sense of rational mind and willful purpose in any endeavor and to social, religious, and cultural identity among many native groups, and sweating represents a continuing manifestation of native religions.

Nez Perce Sweat Lodge

The native American-style sweat lodge produces the same bodily effects as the sauna, but I believe it exposes one to a more holistic relationship with the natural environment. The inter-relationships between earth, air, fire, water, and life are combined and experienced directly. For me, a series of sweats is a beneficial precursor to making important personal decisions, reviewing means for solving problems, and preparing for any major trip or undertaking. Besides the healthful and pleasurable effects, I consider sweating a centering activity—it clears away chaff accumulated from daily existence.

I have been constructing the basic Nez Perce-Umatilla style sweat lodge for personal use and in college field courses for a dozen years now, and I highly recommend it. It's simplicity and versatility make it equally effective for semi-permanent use near one's country, forest, or desert home, or for temporary use on camping and backpacking trips. Provided one has materials for a covering and a half-gallon or larger water container (all additional components are provided by nature), a couple of industrious people can build a lodge and be sweating profusely within two or three hours. A strong and lasting sense of camaraderie quickly develops among friends, old and new, who build a lodge and sweat together.

Constructing a Sweat Lodge

Here are some guidelines for constructing the simple willow-frame sweat lodge. I hope my experiences and the accompanying suggestions help to make your own first sweat lodge a fun, healthy, and memorable endeavor.

The Setting. The ideal location for a sweat lodge is a secluded, grassy meadow or sandbar by a pond or stream with ample willow thickets, firewood, non-explosive heat-retaining rocks, good vibrations, and well away from gawking observers who may not understand. "Ideal" is not mandatory, however; make the best of what is available.

Tiny mountain rivulets can be temporarily dammed to create a pool large enough to sit in, a functional frame can be fashioned from driftwood, etc. The object is to take a sweat the best way you can. Like a sauna, you can build a sweat lodge in your back yard and rinse with a hose or buckets of water, but the essence of the sweat lodge is best experienced in a natural wilderness setting.

NOTE: Many wilderness areas have restrictions on fire-building, especially during summer. Check with local officials to make sure your fire won't bring on an alarm.

The Rocks. Sweat lodge rocks should heat up quickly without crumbling, fracturing, or exploding, and they should retain their heat through two or three consecutive sweats. *Never* use the rounded, stream-worn cobbles so common along watercourses—they frequently retain water which, when heated in a fire, expands more rapidly than the rock does and thus explodes, sending potentially lethal chips flying in all directions. About two dozen heavy, porous, homogeneous rocks of volcanic origin, soft-ball sized or slightly larger, collected away

The ideal location for a sweat lodge is a secluded, grassy meadow or sandbar by a pond or stream with ample willow thickets, firewood, non-explosive heat-retaining rocks, good vibrations, and well away from gawking observers who may not understand.

from open water, streambeds, or seepage areas, are best. Basalt, especially vesicular basalt (with little round holes all over it), is always relia-
ble. Granite and sandstone tend to crumble; quartz and the
crypto-crystalline rocks such as flint and jasper can fracture and send
off glassy flakes.

In the lodge, you can prevent accidents from flying chips by laying a piece of window-screen over the rocks before sprinkling any water
on them. Obviously all potential sweat bathers are not geologists, so
you will have to do some experimenting. I still have no idea what some
of the best rocks I've used actually were.

The Fire. Collect the rocks and build your fire first, so the rocks
will be heating while you construct the lodge. Use an existing firepit
if possible, or build it on a sand (but not gravel) bar, patch of bare dirt,
or some place away from flammable vegetation. (The goal is to have
a good sweat, not to mar the landscape.) The entire fire, rocks included,
is laid before it is ignited. If you are uncertain about the explosive qualities of your rocks, lay the fire fifteen or twenty yards from the lodge
site for safety. Spread a generous amount of kindling (dry grasses, twigs,
bark, dead cones, needles, etc.) on the ground and cover this with a
thick layer of dead wood quite level on the top. Dead pine and fir bark
burn hotter than the wood does. Nestle a bunch of your rocks on the
platform, cover them with another layer of wood, then more rocks, etc.,
until all rocks are in place and you have built a two-and-a-half-foot
square layered pyramid. Lean slabs of bark or heavy sticks upright
around all sides and ignite your small monolith at the bottom. The bark
sidewalls will usually contain any exploding rocks. When the fire has
burned to a pile of coals, in one or two hours, the rocks will be ready.

The Water. Water to be sprinkled on the hot rocks in the lodge is
best warmed first. Hot water does not cool off the rocks as fast. Place
your bucket of water near the fire while the rocks are heating, or drop
a hot rock into the water and stir a few minutes before the sweat.

The Frame. Freshly cut willows are standard for the temporary
sweat lodge frame, but any supple, six-to-ten-foot saplings about an
inch or less in diameter at the butts may be used. Where willow was
non-existant, I have substituted alder, bigleaf and vine maples, red osier
dogwood, mock orange and Oregon myrtle (for a spicy-smelling sweat).
It is important that the shoots be fairly straight and supple—ones that
will bend without snapping. Cut a dozen of these, trim off side branches
and foliage, and sharpen the butts.

To make the dome just the right size (snug, but not cramped) for
the number of people who will use it, seat everyone in a tight circle

and mark the circumference with a few rocks. Remember to leave ample room for the rock pit in the center or to either side of the doorway. An optimum-sized lodge holds four to six people.

Shove the willows a few inches into the ground around the circle, roughly eighteen to twenty-four inches apart so that each corresponds to another directly opposite it. Bend opposites together and inter-twine their ends, or bind them in place with peeled strips of willow bark or

The willows can all cross at the center and be affixed there, or they can be paired and bound into a series of arches running side to side and front to back with many cross points.

other cordage. The willows can all cross at the center and be affixed there, or they can be paired and bound into a series of arches running side to side and front to back with many cross points, but no central point where they all intersect. When bending the willows to shape the dome keep the sides (against which your back will be) as vertical as possible so you won't have to sit and sweat in hunchbacked misery. Keep the dome ceiling low, yet leave adequate headroom—heat will concentrate and be wasted in a high dome.

Two or three rows of smaller willows can be intertwined or tied horizontally around the frame for increased sturdiness and to prevent the coverings from sagging inward. Once the coverings are in place, check inside for other sags and further brace them with small willows. Be sure to remove any sharp stubs that might puncture the covering outside, or your back inside. Leave a two-foot-wide, two-and-a-half-foot-high door space between two of the uprights as you build the frame. I usually tie a sturdy crosspiece in place for the top of the doorway so I can drape a doubled horse blanket over it.

Most native lodges of the open country faced east where the sun rises "pure and clean" each morning. The cardinal directions were less important to the west coast riverine tribes who oriented more to upriver, downriver, toward the river and away from the river; their sweat lodges usually faced the river.

The Pit. Aboriginally, the pit for the hot rocks was dug in the center of the lodge or just inside, to the left or right of the doorway; the preferred position still varies from one culture to the next. Sometimes, in temporary native lodges, the hot rocks were simply piled on the ground or on another large, flat rock. I've found that heat distribution is more even with a central pit (everyone gets the hot rush at the same time), but more care must be exercised in moving in and out of the lodge; a sweat does not feel good on burned human skin. Moving rocks in and out of the lodge is easier if you have the pit by the door, but the back of the lodge sometimes remains cooler. (This can be a plus for novice sweat bathers).

The pit can be dug before or after the frame is erected and should be roughly eighteen inches wide and nearly as deep. To help the rocks retain their heat longer, line the pit with thin, flat slabs of rock (not stream cobbles). Even one large, flattish rock nestled at the bottom of the pit is better than using the plain dirt pit. The flat rock lining also prevents the pit bottom from becoming muddy and the walls from caving in. A viable, though less aesthetic, alternative to using a pit is to fill a metal bucket with the hot rocks, place it in the lodge wherever you want and sprinkle water onto it—kind of like a portable, pre-fab kit.

Lodge Coverings. On a backpacking trip you will have to make do with the tarps, ground cloths, space blankets, plastic sheets, foam pads, extra clothing or whatever else you can dig from your pack. Several layers over the frame are better than just one. I don't like plastic as an initial covering because it is non-absorbent, hot against one's skin, and it's . . . well . . . plastic. If plastic is all you have, use it. As a first layer, it will protect more valuable nylon tarps, tents, etc., laid over it.

Wool blankets, burlap, rugs and rug padding, mattress covers, canvas tarps, old sleeping bags, and quilts piled and layered over the frame to a depth of several inches make the best coverings. A properly finished lodge should be entirely dark inside, well-sealed around the base (heap dirt, sand and rocks around the outside to close any drafts), and have an easily opened but close-fitting doorflap. If the coverings want to slide off, tie or weight them down with rocks set on top of the frame, poles leaned against it, etc. For increased insulation and darkness I have effectively improved single-layered, plastic-covered lodges by literally burying them beneath bark slabs, dirt, leafy branches and boughs, ferns, moss and other vegetation. The only limit to a well-functioning sweat lodge is your own ingenuity.

Aromatics. A sweat lodge built on a grassy spot needs no additional flooring, but one built on dirt, sand, or gravel should be made cleaner, more aromatic, and especially more comfortable for bare bottoms by laying in a floor of leaves (stripped willow leaves work fine), ferns, sage foliage, soft fir boughs, dry or green grass, etc. Aromatic and/or medicinal herbs (many are both) are standard components of the native sweat lodge, whether they comprise the flooring, are soaked in the warm water or used to sprinkle water on the rocks. They can be crumbled directly onto the hot rocks to inhale as smoke.

Grand fir, alpine fir, and the wild mints are commonly used in Umatilla lodges; other people use various sages, junipers, and other confiers. Native ethnographies and ethnobotanies are superb sources to learn what plants were used in your own region. I seldom fail to find some aromatic or medicinal plant growing close to the lodge that is beneficial to a sweat.

Procedures and Suggestions

My sweat with Lem and Michael exemplifies the procedure I normally follow, but some additional thoughts are in order. I was taught always to wet my hair or my whole body before entering the lodge, and always to enter backwards. Wet hair acts as a cooling mechanism, stimulates perspiration, and helps the body adjust more easily to a hotter first sweat.

Native people enter the sweat lodge backwards to prevent evil spirits from sneaking into the lodge behind them. This part of the native ritual is easily understood and practiced; because the sweat lodge is a place for cultivating only positive, constructive attitudes, reminding you to banish hostile or unproductive thoughts and to concentrate on the imminent cleansing, strengthening powers of the lodge.

The sweat is both a personal and a shared experience; be respectful of your fellow bathers. Quiet conversation is acceptable, but loud or harsh words or banal interactions have no place inside the lodge.

For wilderness sweats the hot rocks are flipped from the fire with long sticks and rolled to the lodge, carried on forked sticks, or they can be clamped in bent willow tongs. Nearer to civilization, pitchforks and shovels are commonly used. Be sure to brush coals and ash from the rocks before sealing up the lodge—smoky sweats are no fun.

Water should be only sprinkled, not poured, onto the rocks. The temperature and humidity should increase steadily but gradually, at a pace compatible with all members of the group. The temperature remains cooler at ground level, and those experiencing any breathing difficulty should lower their heads or kneel down. Should anyone express extreme discomfort, it is best they leave the sweat early; some people are susceptible to heat prostration during even a mild sweat. Establish a breathing rhythm and breathe only through your nose during the hottest part of the sweat. An average sweat lasts fifteen to twenty minutes, and ends by everyone's mutual consent.

A Cleansing Process

It is best to experience a series of consecutive sweats—during the first, one's body only begins the cleansing process. The first sweat usually congests my sinuses and lungs, but they totally clear during the second or third. With each succeeding sweat, the body adjusts more rapidly to hotter temperatures, so much so that the first sweat seems lukewarm compared to the third or fourth. Drink water profusely between sweats; your body can use it.

If enough people are present, one person should remain outside the lodge to act as doorman and fireman. His job is to seal closed the door of the lodge for those sweating, to keep the fire going with additional rocks and water heating, pass into the lodge more rocks and water if requested, and to open the door flap when the bathers indicate (whoop) that they are ready to emerge. Appreciation for the doorman's services is often acknowledged with a final sprinkle of water on the rocks in his name at the end of the sweat.

Much aboriginal sweating was done at dawn and was considered the proper way to greet each new day. Nowadays native sweating is more common in late afternoon, at the end of the workday, but a good sweat is worth the effort put into it anytime. A night sweat during a full moon is especially exhilarating.

Keep Mind and Motives Pure

It is, I believe, pretentious for many of us to blindly adopt and profess elements of another culture's traditions, when those traditions reflect a centuries-old lifeway and unique world view that most of us have not directly experienced, nor can truly comprehend. When you make and use your own sweat lodge, incorporate what traditions you can understand, but be mindful of your own ignorance and be respectful of what you are sharing with native American heritage that is beyond your own knowledge. Keep your heart, mind, and motives pure and you will reap the benefits while you establish your own traditions. Lem says it better: "A sweathouse is a place of religion to the Indians. It is a place to gain much wisdom from the Old Ones. It is a place to clean your mind and soul. Always try never to misuse one, and it will always take care of your body and soul."

Happy sweating!

Chapter 15

Bounty of the Wildwood

By Ron (Gus) Gustaveson

*"Let me say right now that fried ant larvae sprinkled with sugar
is one of the most savory foods I have ever tasted."*

Once upon a time . . . as the story goes . . . while I was enjoying a bit of leisure far from the haunts of civilization, I was suddenly seized by a primitive instinct, that raw innate nature that is a part of every wild creature of the woods, whether man or beast.

The blue smoke from my campfire was slowly rising as I leaped across the small creek which dashed and danced over slippery stones, then wound its way far into the valley below. Every creature of the forest was enjoying that same wild, stimulating, solitude and closeness of nature, the rhythm of the wildwood.

The smashing kick of a black boot overturned a log, revealing an array of worker and "nursemaid" ants (of the red and black variety) which, in an effort to preserve their precious larvae and possibly their lives, quickly scurried about as if some impending danger was hastening their doom.

Had you been present at this scene, you would have undoubtedly heard the scraping sound of a large tin bucket as it scooped up dirt, twigs, ants, and larvae.

Separating the larvae from the rest was a time-consuming process. First I added water to the half-filled bucket and stirred it. The worker and nursemaid ants (which devotedly clung to their larvae) and the twigs floated to the surface where they could be skimmed from the water into a tin wash dish. Next I poured clean water into the wash dish and repeated the process several times.

Stirring caused the sticks to seperate from the ants, and the larvae often came loose from the grasp of the nursemaids and bunched up before I spooned them out.

The blue smoke continued to rise as I molded and pressed the larvae into the shape of a small hamburger patty. The hot grease popped as I pitched the delicacy into the smoking frying pan.

I leaned against a clump of small chokecherry trees. "Ah," I thought, "this is the life!"

The savory, sweet smell of the golden brown patty released a luscious mouth-watering aroma as it sizzled in the grease. I relaxed and lost myself in my book.

When I make a semi-permanent camp, I always try to have a little sugar on hand for various reasons, so when the patty was golden brown, a little of the sugar was sprinkled on top for unparalleled excellence.

Let me say right now that fried ant larvae, sprinkled with sugar, is one of the most savory foods I have ever tasted, regardless of origin. You have propably tasted rice-crispy balls, chewed their sweet kernels, consumed their sweet nuggets with delight, yet how many of us have noticed the similarity between rice-crispy balls and fried ant larvae?

Futhermore, the strength imparted by such a snack will leave you nothing short of astonished!

I know you will want to experiment with your own delectable recipes at the first opportunity. Let me encourage you to make them a permanent part of your survival knowledge. The delightful flavor, once experienced, will stick in a wrinkle of your brain where it can be immediately recalled at the first sight of an ant hill.

Few readers will believe this. How unfortunate it is that man has removed himself so far from the natural world and the enjoyment of the bounties of nature.

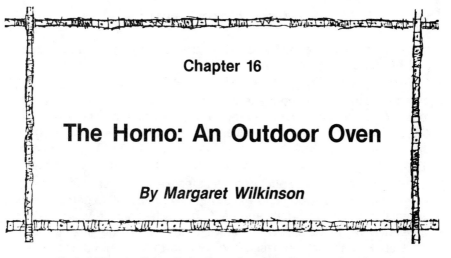

Chapter 16

The Horno: An Outdoor Oven

By Margaret Wilkinson

"In addition to the satisfaction of completing a project from beginning to end, I believe this new skill could be quite useful in case of an emergency, to make a bad situation a bit easier."

We pulled into the camp about 9:00 a.m. Monday, unloaded our gear and pitched our lean-to. My husband, Ernie, took off immediately to prepare for his teaching assignment and I commandeered another instructor to help me collect several buckets of the red clay native to that part of the country.

I had been waiting for a long time to build a clay oven, but I just never could find time with all my usual activities at home. I determined that if I didn't accomplish one other thing at the Woodsmoke Rendezvous this year, I would try my hand at constructing a horno.

We live in the San Luis Valley in southwestern Colorado, an area rich in Spanish traditions and customs, so many of our neighbors have hornos near their houses and they use them regularly for baking. This skill has fascinated me for some time so I thoroughly questioned one of my Spanish friends who builds hornos for other people for the information I needed.

I was told that the clay should be washed and cleaned of rocks, sticks, and grasses so it won't explode when it is heated, and that by mixing the red and green clays native to that area I would have better adhesion—advice I decided to forego in favor of getting started right away since it takes several days for the clay to dry well enough to fire without cracking.

To Begin the Horno

First the ground had to be cleared and leveled and the soil loosened. Next, I gathered enough flat, oval-shaped rocks for the floor and to line the side wall of the horno to hold the heat during baking. I embedded the stones in the loose dirt.

With the foundation laid, I mixed enough water into a large pan of red clay to make it workable and mortared the rocks in place. This made the oven floor smooth so my pans would lay flat and slide in and out easily. Next I put a thick layer of clay around the outside of the oven floor and worked the edges of larger rocks into the clay to give them a firm base. Then I smoothed clay on both sides of the rocks.

Once the floor was built, the next step was to construct the dome. We were in a cottonwood and willow area so I was able to gather plenty of small cottonwood sticks and bark. First a few curved willow sticks were anchored in the clay layer between the floor and outside ring, then more sticks were criss-crossed back and forth to form a dome shape. The small sticks wouldn't hold much weight so I used plenty of bark to build up the inside of the dome. This would give extra support once the heavy layer of clay was in place.

By this time I was getting some pretty incredulous stares from passers-by. One or two even asked what in the world I was doing. They didn't know much more when I told them I was "building a horno." They would just have to wait for the final results.

Forming the Chimney

Most hornos come to a peak with a chimney hole at the top. I wanted mine to be dome-shaped with the chimney at the back. To form the chimney I gathered some straight sticks and tied them into a bundle with cottonwood bark. As I began covering the dome with mud, I wedged the bundle into the back of the dome and worked the clay over it to form the chimney. At this point I mortared the sides and top thoroughly, leaving an opening at the front for the doorway.

Because I built the horno in the sun, I was concerned that it would dry more quickly than it should and the clay would crack, but I only had four days for this drying to take place. If you have plenty of time I would recommend that you build your oven in a shady spot so it can dry more gradually.

Drying Process

As the clay dried, it could eventually support it's own weight. A few of the center sticks were carefully pulled out so the air could circulate better and speed up the drying process. At first I tried to patch

"... I was getting pretty incredulous stares from passers-by, one or two even asked what I was doing, but they didn't know much more when I answered that I was "building a horno.""

up cracks with more clay as they appeared, but my busy schedule didn't leave time for repairs.

The "hour of reckoning" came after breakfast on the last morning of the Rendezvous. I was afraid of what might happen when the oven was fired. I wasn't sure the drying process was complete and I was afraid it might just blow up when the moisture expanded in the heat.

I took one of the blazing sticks of wood from the campfire and put it inside the oven. My husband, Ernie, and our son, Larry, and I exchanged anxious glances as the willow arches and cottonwood inside the oven caught fire, smoke billowed from the chimney and cracks. It held.

Larry and I quickly mixed up extra clay and began to patch some of the larger cracks. By now the oven was too hot to touch so we used sticks to work the mortar into the crevices. The heat seemed to help the wet clay adhere to the oven and we were convinced that it would hold together after all. I can't explain my exuberance. It was exciting to see that my horno was actually going to work. All I could say was, "Whoopee!" . . . a reaction shared by everyone who had been following the project.

I kept a fire going to get the rocks good and hot while I mixed sourdough fruit bread. Larry gathered green willows to lay on top of the hot stones on the oven floor. This would keep the bottom of the bread from burning.

I pulled out the coals and ashes with a small shovel. Then I put the green willows on the oven floor and set the pan of fruit bread in the center of the oven. A few pre-heated flat rocks were used to cover the oven door and the opening on top of the chimney to prevent too much heat from escaping.

This was exciting. I couldn't help but peek into the oven a time or two to check the rising process, but I saw that the bread was browning too fast. To regulate the heat, I moved one of the stones in the doorway a little and partially opened the chimney. After about fifteen minutes I replaced the stones to retain heat and allow slow cooking.

Golden Brown Bread

Forty-five minutes later I lifted a loaf of golden brown, perfectly raised bread from my horno. I couldn't have been more pleased. Although I found when I cut the bread that one corner had burned slightly, I really couldn't have done better in my electric oven at home. I cut the loaf into small pieces and almost everyone had a taste.

The loaf of sourdough fruit bread was placed in the oven on green willow sticks to keep it from burning on the bottom.

As instructors we sometimes get so caught up in the skills we are teaching we don't have time to "experiment" on our own new projects, but this Rendezvous was a real success for me. As usual, we had shared skills with other instructors, but I had had an opportunity to "experiment" on a project I had planned for some time. This made my trip very satisfying.

I learned that it wasn't necessary to use the refined clay used for pottery. Since then I have built other larger ovens and with thicker walls. They hold the heat longer so more than one baking can be done with each firing. After the initial firing, it helps to brush out the inside of the cooled oven so that small pieces of ash from the burned arches won't drop into the food as it cooks. In addition to the satisfaction I experienced by completing a project totally from beginning to end, I believe this new skill could be quite useful in an emergency. Building a horno oven could make a bad situation a bit easier.

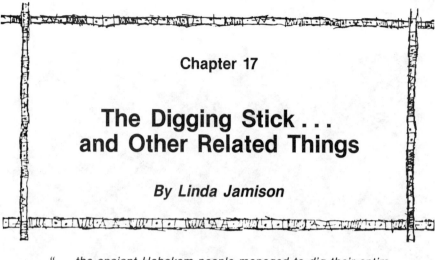

Chapter 17

The Digging Stick...
and Other Related Things

By Linda Jamison

*"... the ancient Hohokam people managed to dig their entire
water irrigation system—some ditches measuring up to
fifteen feet wide—with only digging sticks."*

The vernal equinox awakens my urge to forage. Of course, to find tender roots and shoots this time of year one must "dig" a little. I mean that literally—but first things first.

To dig for roots, you must have a digging stick. You could use a shovel, but for a modern-day aborigine to use a shovel would be really barbarous. If you made a digging stick last year and stored it out of the weather, it will probably still be serviceable this year. If not, spring is the ideal time to make one.

The digging stick is a most important tool of primitive life—modern-day or ancient. It can be used as an implement for digging root foods as well as for a shovel. It is interesting to note that the early Hohokam people managed to dig their entire water irrigation system—some ditches measuring up to fifteen feet wide—using only digging sticks.

Constructing such a tool may sound like a simple task; just find a stick and use it for digging, right?

Wrong!

A digging stick must meet certain criteria. First, it must be strong enough to pry out roots without breaking. This means a stick at least two inches in diameter. For maximum strength it should be cut green, peeled and shaved smooth, sharpened, and then fire-hardened. Medium-hard woods such as chokecherry (Prunus virginiana) are best, but willow (Salix) can also be transformed into a good digging stick.

The digging stick should be long enough to give good leverage— the longer the stick, the more leverage you will have.

The second requirement is length. For proper leverage the stick should be a minimum of three feet long, and the longer the stick the better leverage you will have.

Third, the stick must have a sharp digging edge. A spatula- shaped end will make digging easier and allow the edge to cut through the soil closer to the root. A comfortable, rounded handle will also make digging easier and give you more control.

A well-made digging stick will last many months with only occasional sharpening. You may want to carve your own embellishments onto the tool, such as your name or original designs, because a good, unclaimed digging stick will disappear quickly.

Other Related Things

Now that you have the implement, what you will dig? How about those odoriferous offerings of spring, wild onions (Allium). They are among the first to show their slender tops, and if you made a note of their general location last year, you will know exactly where to begin searching now.

When you spot a clump protruding conspicuously from the still-bare earth, plunge your digging stick deep into the ground about two or three inches from the plant. Remember, these are "wild" herbs. To absorb sufficient water from the soil, they must stretch their roots more deeply than do the ordinary garden variety. Therefore, you must push the tip of your stick deep enough to pry the plant out of the ground without breaking off the bulb. Mastering this technique will save the time it takes to "shovel" it out with your stick.

Since I have suggested that you choose the wild onion as a source of digging experimentation, I must also assume the responsibility of warning you about it's virulent look-alike . . . death camas (Zygadenus gramineus).

Death camas grows, in it's various forms, from Canada to Florida, Texas, New Mexico, Arizona, and California.

Alas, a thorn on the rose (if you can compare an onion to a rose): the death camas grows in much the same locale as the wild onion does, and the untrained eye could easily fail to distinguish between the two.

Further study of the flower clusters in the summer will eliminate the indiscriminate gathering of death camas. The greenish-white to yellowish-white colored elongated clusters of the death camas are quite different from the rose-to-whitish umbel flowers of the wild onion.

Once it blooms, it is far easier to differentiate between death camas and other similar-looking plants such as sego lily (Calochortus) camass (Camassia) and the wild onion or garlic.

Some so-called "experts" recommend that you try the taste test—granted, nothing I know of tastes quite like wild onion or garlic. In fact,

This deceptive bulb is death camas; one bite could kill an adult. In the spring there is no flower, which makes positive identification difficult.

I once took a clump of the "little stinkers" to a plant identification lecture I was giving. Everyone good-naturedly tasted one and we had to open the window to continue the class.

What I am saying is, this strong odor *can* help you identify the real thing, but beware—when you are collecting wild onions your hands will become tainted and everything you pick up will carry the odor so you won't be able to recognize which of the plants smell and which do not.

The similarity between death camas (left) and wild onion (right) is evident, but an unknowing forager might mistake them when they are found growing on the same terrain.

Tasting some plants may help you identify them as well, but a small bite of the wrong plant might also prove fatal. Death camas contains a substance called "Zygadenine," an alkaloid whose effect is twice as toxic as strychnine.

The symptoms of poisoning from death camas are; salavation, weakness, lowering of the body temperature, nausea, and finally coma. If you suspect that someone has eaten this plant, by all means encourage free vomiting and get the sick person to a doctor as soon as possible. (If this is not possible, and you have the supplies available, keep the victim as quiet as possible and administer a solution of water and baking soda orally.)

So what is the answer?

When gathering wild onions or garlic the body picks up the odor and everything you collect takes on the pungent smell.

Study. You must become aware of the appearance of edible *and* poisonous plants in their various stages of growth to avoid a serious mistake.

It took many years of study before I learned to recognize the v-shaped groove in the narrow, grass-like leaf of the death camas as opposed to the nearly round, wild onion leaf.

Other Spring Look-Alikes

There are other formidable early spring look-alikes. For instance, poisonous hemlock (Conium maculatum) is almost identical to wild carrot (Daucus carota) in its early stages, and poisonous dogbane (Apocynum cannabinum) is barely distinguishable from milkweed (Asclepias speciosa) when only the young shoots are visible.

My point is, only regular study will assure your safe enjoyment of spring foraging. Don't take short cuts.

Well, as you can see, one thing has led to another. It is sometimes hard to cover one subject without converging into other related areas. But, that's the way nature is—one exciting discovery leads to another, and another, and another. Before you realize it, you are totally immersed.

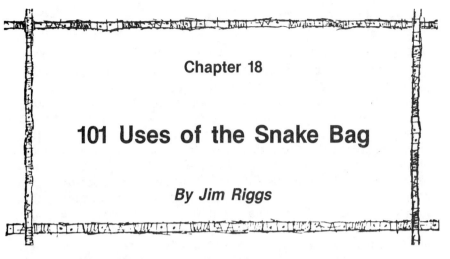

Chapter 18

101 Uses of the Snake Bag

By Jim Riggs

"While I now prefer to observe reptiles and amphibians in their natural habitats, and rarely carry any home in my trusty snake bag, the bag remains essential to any outing."

In junior high school I became eagerly engaged in the study of herpetology (reptiles and amphibians). I soon learned, from peers and from reading, that the prescribed method for carrying these cold-blooded critters after they were collected in the field was in cloth bags, from pillow-size on down. I seldom ventured into the woods without one or two of these bags tucked under my belt.

A budding young herpetologist does not always return from a collecting trip with his snake bags bulging with squirming creatures, but I seldom returned without something to show for my time . . . rocks, moss to line a terrarium, ants or termites to feed my lizards and turtles, mint or yerba buena for tea, and many other treasures to be found in nature: Once it was a highly odoriferous vulture egg collected from a cave, months after the nesting season.

My snake bag was the obvious container in which to carry all these important findings.

Conversely, at the beginning of a hike, the same bag was handy for carrying an orange or candy bar, small notebook and pencil for recording data, extra film, and any number of other necessary articles too bulky to fit in a pocket, or too slippery to stay in the pocket of one who was continually bending over to look under rocks, bark, and dead logs for the sought-after quarry.

In those early days my friends and I depended on our mothers to sew up some bags for us occasionally. But soon our demands far exceeded what our mothers were willing to supply, and we were forced to learn the intricacies of a sewing machine to produce our own.

Designed for securely holding such determined escape artists as snakes, snake bags have two main requirements; they should be long enough so that the top portion can be tied in an overhand knot, and all the seams should be double-stitched. Unbleached muslin, because it is durable, cheap, and "breathes," is the most commonly used material although I have a friend who once decided that muslin bags were too dull and un-inspiring for the truly dedicated herpetologist—he began to mass-produce brightly colored paisley bags. Not to be quietly outdone, I got a bunch of muslin bags and tie-died them into my own bright patterns.

Over the years snake bags have served as emergency bandages, bandannas, potholders, washcloths, towels, flags, pads for uncomfortable pack straps, and all-around ditty bags. I've used them for leaching the tannic acid from freshly ground acorn meal in a stream, collecting innumerable wild foods, and for keeping fish moist and fresh (and safe from bands of marauding crayfish).

While I now prefer to observe reptiles and amphibians in their natural habitats, and rarely carry any home in my trusty snake bag, the bag remains essential to any outing. Snake bags have proven their usefulness to me far beyond their intended function, and they have infiltrated the ranks of many friends who wouldn't think of catching snakes.

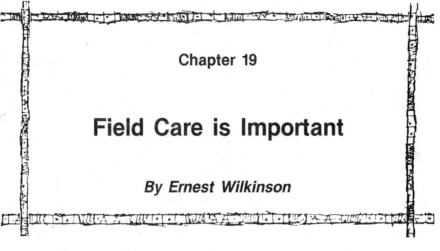

Chapter 19

Field Care is Important

By Ernest Wilkinson

"The most important thing to remember is to get the animal dressed out and the heat removed as soon after the kill as possible."

Much good meat spoils and goes to waste each year, not necessarily from warm weather, but from improper preparation and handling. This mainly applies to the game meat taken each fall by hunters who are not familiar with the care of meat in the field, nor do rural people always know the right way to butcher and care for beef, goats, and other domestic animals. Suggestions that follow on the care of meat apply equally to wild game and to domestically raised animals.

First, don't run the animal before dropping it for butchering: a heated animal makes tough meat. The same principle applies to deer, elk, and other game that has been run from ridge to ridge by other hunters before it is killed.

After you have killed the animal, remove the intestines immediately. Prop the cavity open to let the heat escape. Cooling the carcass during this first hour or so can be very important to the future storage and edibility of the meat.

Generally, when you butcher a domestic animal, you have the equipment ready for the job, so I will steer my comments toward game animals taken during hunting season when you might have to improvise according to weather conditions, available equipment, and other factors. The same general principles can also apply to domestic animals.

The process of dressing or gutting an animal is basically the same—cut the skin open from the anus to the throat and pull out the wind pipe and gullet, lungs, heart, liver, stomach, and the complete intestinal tract. Take particular care not to puncture any of the intestines because fluids might drain onto the meat and start spoilage. Cut away or clean any bloody spots. Early spoilage sometimes gets started in these areas. A cloth carried in your pocket can be used for this purpose or rub a handful of snow on the area and brush it away. This does a good job during winter.

If you can't start cutting up the carcass or move it out to storage right away, remove the insides and prop the cavity open with sticks so that the body heat can escape. If the weather is warm, don't leave the carcass exposed to the sun. This defeats the cooling process. If your kill is a deer, or similar-sized animal, you can usually drag it to the shade of a tree or brush. If it is a larger animal such as an elk, gather some old snags and broken tree limbs and form them into a rough tipi-shape over the carcass. Cover the stick frame with boughs, grass, or whatever you can find to create shade. This allows the air to circulate under the shade frame for cooling. It will also keep the birds away from the meat.

Meat Storage

Cooling a large game animal can be helped along by skinning it and then cutting it into quarters to hang, or by laying it out on a rock, or a log, in the shade. If flies are still moving about during midday, you may have to stay by the meat and swish them off with a willow or evergreen bough. Then, when the sun goes down and the flies quit moving, you can go back to camp and return in the morning before sunup to pack the cooled meat out to storage.

In addition to standard refrigeration, there are many ways to store meat for later use. In cool, mountainous country, hang the meat in a shady area. Wrap each piece in cloth, blankets, tarps or similar material to keep the meat cool and protect it from flies. At night take all wrappings off to let the cool night air circulate around it. Then, before sunup, wrap it again. By repeating this process daily, properly dressed and cooled meat can be kept in edible condition for many days, depending on the time of year, temperature, and other factors, of course.

If the meat is to be cut up and frozen, I prefer to let the carcass hang in a cool place for several days to age before it is frozen. This makes the meat more tender.

The most important thing to remember: get the animal dressed out and the heat removed as soon after the kill as possible. Then keep the meat clean, cool, out of the sun, and the flies away from it. *Do not* wrap meat in plastic or other non-porous material or it will spoil very quickly from lack of circulation. *Do not* leave a carcass on the ground overnight. Hang the meat or prop it off the ground with sticks or rocks so that air can circulate freely around the animal. *Do not* attempt to carry meat in the closed trunk of a car on a hot day—it can sour in an hour or two under such conditions.

Proper Care

When skinning the animal, remember that the hide is very useful if it is properly cared for. It takes as much time and effort to tan a poor hide as it does a good one, so use care during the skinning. You don't want to end up with knife marks and holes. After the skin is removed from the animal, trim off excess fat and remaining meat, lay it out flat in the shade and sprinkle salt on the flesh side. Be sure to cover all areas and flatten any wrinkles. It can then be rolled, flesh side in, for storage until tanning.

Pelts on stretchers: (left to right) badger, beaver, coyote, bobcat, raccoon.

If the weather, or other conditions, do not allow storing the meat, and if no freezer is available, it can be home canned in glass jars, or cut into thin strips and dried for jerky. But no matter how you choose to store the game for later use, remember that it can be no better than the care and the immediate cooling it receives in the field.

Animal fur and hides have always been an important part of man's survival, especially for primitive man. Fur and hides were used as items of clothing and they also had a part in tool making. For instance, rawhide (hide with the hair removed) was known as "Indian iron" which had many uses such as in strips for lashings or for drumheads.

Modern man has carried over these uses in luxurious fur coats, fur-lined parkas, shoes and boots, belts and other garments and accessories.

Of course to obtain top market value for them, the first step is proper care of the animal skins or pelts in the field or the drying shed. This will also give a good quality fur or leather if you plan to tan the skins and pelts yourself, or take them to a tannery.

Do not skin out a pelt and throw the fresh hide into a corner for several days until you get around to it. A fresh hide can gather mildew, hair slip and be worthless if it isn't stretched out to dry without wrinkles.

In addition to obtaining the animal and caring for the meat in the right way, proper skinning is necessary, especially if you intend to sell the furs to a fur buyer. For example, if you cut a coyote, fox, or bobcat down the belly for skinning, very few commercial fur buyers would buy it. Even if they did, the price would be far below market. The reason for this is that most garment makers would use the white belly-fur in one type of garment and the back fur in another. If you cut the skin down the belly during the skinning process, the white fur is only half as wide as it should be.

Remember that animals do not wear their overcoat during the hot summer months any more than you and I do. If you are utilizing hides for the fur, they will be of little use during the warm months. They will be thick and luxurious during cold winters. Don't let that natural resource go to waste.

Your first attempt at skinning an animal will probably be rather time-consuming, but with practice and experience you will learn to jerk the pelt off a bobcat in about five minutes—a muskrat in a minute.

If you intend to tan—or have the hides tanned—for your own use, simply lay the skinned hide out flat in a cool, shady area and rub salt into all areas of the skin. Fatty hides, such as raccoon and skunk, should be placed over a round fleshing beam or log and the excess fat scraped, or trimmed off with a draw knife or similar tool before salting. If you intend to sell the furs on the raw fur market do not salt them. Instead, flesh off excess tissue and fat from the pelt, then put it on the proper stretcher for that animal and allow the hide to dry in a cool place.

Skinning the Animal

Before skinning the animal, determine whether the fur is to be stretched and dried for the raw fur market or whether it will be tanned for your own use. In that case, split the hide down the belly so it will lay flat, then salt it. If you plan to sell the furs of the fox, coyote, bobcat, raccoon or skunk, they should be skinned cased. To case the skins, you must make the opening cuts down the back of each hind leg, to and around the anus, and down the tail on the underside.

Using a sharp knife get the hide started at the legs, then hang the carcass by the hind legs. Pull the skin down over it just like pulling a sleeve inside out.

On the short tail of a bobcat, you must cut it the full length on the underside. Then carefully—because it is a rather tender, fatty texture—remove the tail bone. For fox or coyote, slit the tail open a few inches. Work the skin loose from the tail base, then slip in a couple of small sticks to hold onto. Grasp the tail bone and pull until the bone slips out, leaving a hollow tail. Slip the blade of your knife into this tube and slit it open so the air can get in to dry the skin before the hair slips (falls out).

Don't be concerned about a small amount of fat and membrane that might stick to the skin as you pull it down over the carcass. You might have to use your knife a bit where larger pieces of meat might start to strip down with the skin. Excess fat from fox, coyote, and bobcat can be pulled or scraped off rather easily after the hide is on the stretcher. The fatty hides of raccoons and skunk should be scraped off over a fleshing beam before stretching.

When you skin an animal whose hide will be put on a stretcher, the front legs can be split open on the underside from the foot to within several inches of the body. As you pull the skin down it will slip over the legs more easily. For the fur market, you can cut the leg skin off just above the foot, but if you plan to use the hide yourself, for a floor covering or for a blanket, you might prefer to skin the feet completely out to the toenails.

As you pull the skin off over the head, be careful as you cut through the cartilage at the base of the ears and around the eyes and lips. A

When skinning a fox, coyote or bobcat (shown), the hide is peeled off like a glove without splitting it down the belly.

Fatty raccoon and skunk hides are best fleshed on a beam before stretching.

nice smooth skin without a lot of knife marks and cuts makes a better impression on the fur buyer than one full of holes and blemishes.

After the Animal Is Skinned

After you have skinned the animal, pull the skin down over a wooden or wire frame as shown in the photographs. Pull the hind legs down on the stretcher and fasten them, then widen the stretcher until the skin is fairly tight and let it dry for several hours, or until it is damp-dry.

Once the skin has dried somewhat, but is still pliable, take it off the stretcher and turn it fur-side out. Slip it back onto the stretcher, fasten the hind legs tight again, and let it dry out of the sun for several days.

A raccoon or skunk hide should also be skinned cased, but after scraping off the fat, leave it to dry on the stretcher with the flesh side out. Muskrat, mink, and martin are skinned cased, then fleshed and pulled down over the stretcher with the flesh side out and left to dry

Once the beaver is fleshed, tack the hide to a flat surface or lace it onto a round hoop to dry.

that way. A beaver is split open down the belly from chin to tail and skinned open. Do not cut open from the legs to the center line down the belly. Pull the legs through during the skinning process, but leave a small, round hole. This is best done by cutting the foot off at the joint when you begin so the skin can be slipped over and off the leg more easily.

Beaver skin does not pull off as does a bobcat or coyote: you have to skin the entire surface. I prefer to use a sharp knife and skin clean as I go without any fat or meat left on the pelt rather than rough skinning it and then having to put it on a fleshing beam to scrape the hide clean before stretching. This is an individual choice and some trial and error will help you decide which is best for you.

Once a beaver is skinned and fleshed, it should be stretched in an open, round shape either by tacking it out on a flat surface or by lacing it onto a round hoop of willow.

Badger is skinned open with opening cuts from each foot to the center cut down the belly. The skin is then fleshed and stretched flat in an almost square shape.

If you intend to tan the furs yourself you can eliminate the stretching process by spreading them out flat and rubbing salt into all parts of the hide. If you aren't sure whether you will tan the furs or sell them, they can all be stretched. Then, if you decide to tan them, they can be soaked until soft and then tanned.

Photos by Ernest and Margaret Wilkinson

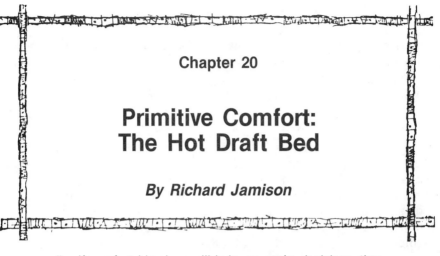

Chapter 20

Primitive Comfort: The Hot Draft Bed

By Richard Jamison

*". . . if comfortable sleep will help you make decisions, then
building a hot draft bed is worth the energy needed
for its construction."*

It was an unusually hot spring for March. I had spent the morning teaching ten students how to dig hot draft beds and we were exhausted—our meager survival diet of ash cakes and biscuit root didn't provide enough energy for such tedious labor. The rest of the day we spent in the shade of a giant cottonwood.

Everyone was anxious to test "the system" against the chill of the desert night. Anticipation grew as the sun went down. Fires had been lit in the pits earlier to dry the soil and drive out any unwelcome denizens, so the ground was warm. We spread thick layers of sage bark over the insulating dirt, banked the fires, and crawled on top of the beds in groups of three and four.

The sensation was strange. We had been huddling between our shelters and sleeping fires for five nights. We were accustomed to the friendly crackle and sweet smell of burning juniper and the familiar glow of flames. Now we had heat, more heat than we had bargained for, without constantly feeding our fires and swatting burning embers off our blankets. We sank quickly into a deep, restful sleep.

About midnight I awoke to much mumbling and commotion. Someone had opened the draft to the maximum, and the rocks and earth had overheated. Now three students were strolling around the campsite looking for a comfortable place to "cool off". They returned to the warm beds just in time for the dreaded 3 a.m. chill.

I built a hot draft bed for the first time about ten years ago. It was pretty much a trial and error project because, although I had seen drawings, I didn't know anyone who had actually built one, but it seemed like a worthy project. Now, after years of experimenting, I can enjoy a new level of comfort on those cold spring nights as a result of this rather unique bit of technology.

Warm Rest Is Important

First, let me say that it would be a waste of time to build a draft bed if you plan to move your camp every night. But if you plan to set up a base camp, and the weather indicates the need, a draft bed is an excellent way to assure a warm, comfortable night. As with most rules, there are exceptions. If you are caught without any protection from the elements (blanket, sleeping bag, jacket, etc.) and expect the temperature to drop drastically during the night a draft bed would be needed. This does happen often in the desert (and in other places), especially in early spring and late fall. Under such circumstances, I wouldn't hesitate to expend the energy and time needed to build a draft bed.

Also, you must decide whether extra warmth is a reasonable trade-off for the amount of energy you will use in its construction. On the other hand, if you are concerned about energy output, consider the energy wasted by shivering all night.

Rest is a very important factor in survival; the body needs proper rest for the mind to function creatively, and survival is a succession of creative decisions. In a nutshell, if comfortable sleep will help you make decisions, then building a hot draft bed is worth the energy needed for its construction.

If you decide to build a hot draft bed, your first step is to choose an appropriate campsite. Naturally you don't want to haul dozens of rocks for miles, so it is important to choose an area where there are plenty of building materials available and, although you will need water to mix the mud mortar for your chimney, be careful not to dig in an area where the ground-water level is high.

The condition of the soil is also very important; extremely rocky, hard soil is not suitable for digging trenches unless you have shovels or other equipment. Assume that you will have no gear, then anything you come up with will be icing on the cake, making the job that much easier.

Ideally (if there is an ideal survival situation), the ground will be solid, yet soft enough to dig easily with a digging stick. There should be plenty of medium-sized flat rocks nearby, and there should be firewood and water within easy carrying distance.

Once these "technical" considerations have been met, another problem might come up—local denizens. I must confess that I have never built a hot draft bed without being bitten by a seething scorpion or a battalion of irate red ants. But if someone dug up my abode I would probably be mad enough to bite, too. The best way to avoid trouble is to tuck your pant legs into your socks while you are digging and check the area carefully. You wouldn't picnic on an ant hill—why would you want to sleep on one?

Select the Right Spot

Let's assume you have picked your ideal spot—sans scorpions, ants and other creeping things—and you have a digging stick. Right? Wrong? If you don't have a digging stick first read the chapter in this book on how to make one. If you have a shovel or a large tin can (and if you are not a purist), by all means use them.

Next, consider the number of people who will be sleeping on this draft bed. One person would build a one-or-two-trench draft system and three can fit comfortably on a three-trench bed. If I am alone in a

Mark out an area the size of the desired draft system, allow room for fire pit and chimney.

survival situation I don't hesitate to build a draft bed myself, if conditions warrant, but with two or three people to help, the digging and carrying process is much faster.

It is important to map out an area for your draft bed so you won't spend valuable time and effort only to find that you've miscalculated and find a tree, bush, or boulder in your path. Figure out the ultimate space you will need to build a three-trench draft bed—about the size of a two-man tent, or the width of a double bed. As for length, you will have a fire pit at one end and a chimney at the other end, so the length will be about four feet longer than the tallest person using the bed. If you have doubts, have someone lie down. Measure them from head to toe then add an extra two feet on each end.

Now you're ready to begin. If you are going to build a three- trench draft bed, dig three trenches about six inches wide and six to eight inches deep. The trenches should be straight except at each end where they will form a junction.

Next, select rocks that will fit flat across the trenches. I have occasionally used rocks to line the trenches also, when the soil was not

Large, flat rocks are laid on top of the trenches. Make sure they fit well over the edges, so they won't collapse.

firm enough to support the rocks and would have collapsed if I had not. This is something to consider in extremely cold weather as well; rock-lined trenches hold the heat longer. But ordinarily I just cover the trenches with the flat rocks, making sure they are wide enough to fit well over the lip of the trench and won't collapse when dirt is piled on top, or someone lays on it.

A chimney is made by stacking rocks in a circular "bricked" manner. After the rock chimney is assembled to a height of three or four feet, it is mortared with mud "cement."

Chimney and Fire

The chimney is built next by cementing rocks with mud. The base, wide at the bottom, will connect with one end of the trenches and slope into a stack with a hole six inches or more in diameter. To keep the smoke above your bed the chimney should be at least four feet high, even higher if you build a shelter over it.

On the other end of the trenches dig a fire pit about two feet by three feet and eight inches deeper than the trenches that will open into the pit. To one side, dig out a section that slopes into the pit. This will allow proper air flow.

Finally, cover the pit by stacking rocks in a dome, or igloo, fashion and cement them with mud so there are no air holes. Once you light a fire in the pit you can see where the smoke escapes, then you can patch up any holes with mud, dirt, bark, or rocks so the structure is practically air tight. A damper, of sorts, can be made by closing or opening the air flow with additional rocks.

Just as you sometimes have trouble getting your fireplace at home to draft, you may have trouble when you first light your draft bed because the chimney and trenches will be cold. This can be rectified by building a fire directly behind the chimney to heat it, then allowing it to burn out as your draft system begins to work.

The last step is to cover the rocks with dirt and other insulating material such as bark, boughs, dry leaves, etc. Use enough to protect you from the hot rocks.

On the first use of your draft beds, it is necessary to light the fire early in the day to thoroughly dry the moist soil and to chase away any small, biting creatures that might be waiting for you to snuggle in for the night. If the ground isn't completely dried out the dampness will be very uncomfortable. Once the ground and rocks are heated the warmth will be easy to maintain through the night. On following nights you can ignite the fires just early enough to build up a good bed of coals, the ground should be dry from the previous night's heat.

If you have ever used wood for heat you can appreciate the difference between the warmth from a fireplace and heat from a good wood stove. A few years ago we lived in an old farmhouse in Montana where we used wood heat exclusively. There was no electric or gas heat back-up system and we quickly learned to judge the amount of wood to stock-pile for a season of cold weather. One winter the temperatures remained below minus twenty degrees from November to April and we burned a cord of wood a week to stay warm. The experience taught me a lot about banking a wood stove and the benefits of a damper system, and I've found that maintaining a hot draft bed is much the same.

Maintaining Your Fire

It takes a *lot* of wood to stay warm next to a sleeping fire, even more on cold nights. If you are trying to maintain two fires and sleep between them, you have to gather twice as much wood. Banking a fire next to a rock or other reflector helps, but you still will burn far more wood than is used in a hot draft bed system.

A fire should be ignited in the pit and allowed to burn for several hours to dry the soil and drive out insects.

A simple "A-frame" shelter can be built over the draft bed for maximum comfort and warmth.

Once the ground is heated you can bank your fire. Load it up and allow a good bed of coals to form, then pile on large pieces of wood. The coals will continue to smolder which will burn the wood more slowly, so that you will only have to add wood once during the night.

During long-term use, some dirt may drift into the trenches and repairs may be necessary; you will find breaks if you watch for escaping smoke when you stoke up the fire pit.

For a really comfortable, warm wilderness camp build an A- frame shelter over your draft bed. Be sure the chimney is higher than the shelter so that it will carry the smoke away.

A Word of Warning

A word of warning—if you come back to an old camp and draft bed be very careful. The trenches make excellent hiding places for small creatures. I once returned to a camp after several days absence to find a rattlesnake enjoying the cool refuge of my underground tunnels. On

Rising heat will warm the inside of your shelter while the canopy keeps you dry and secure from rain or snow.

the day I returned to my camp we began to make repairs and we found the snake when we lifted one of the flat rocks that covered the trench.

Speaking of snakes, let me add another small word of advice: when you lift a rock to repair your tunnels, or for any reason, stand behind it and lift as though it were hinged. The opening side will be away from you. You can then look carefully from the protection of the rock and you will reduce the chance of being bitten as well as avoid surprises. If you do find a snake under the rock drop it quickly and move back.

If the snake is faster than you are, it will move out from under the rock and slither off in the opposite direction.

The best way to avoid this is to light your fires and let them burn for a couple of hours before you make repairs. This should clear out insects, reptiles, and other small inhabitants.

Once you have used a hot draft bed you won't be satisfied on cold nights without one. It's like getting used to an electric blanket— wilderness style. Who said you can't experience quality of life under primitive conditions.

Index